Practicing Intersubjectively

Practicing
Intersubjectively

Peter Buirski

JASON ARONSON
Lanham • Boulder • New York • Toronto • Plymouth, UK

Published in the United States of America
by Jason Aronson
An imprint of Rowman & Littlefield Publishers, Inc.

A wholly owned subsidiary of
The Rowman & Littlefield Publishing Group, Inc.
4501 Forbes Boulevard, Suite 200, Lanham, Maryland 20706
www.rowmanlittlefield.com

Estover Road
Plymouth PL6 7PY
United Kingdom

British Library Cataloguing in Publication Information Available

The hardback edition of this book was previously catalogued by the Library of Congress
as follows:

Buirski, Peter.
    Practicing intersubjectively / Peter Buirski.
        p. cm.
    Includes bibliographical references and index.
    1. Intersubjectively. 2. Psychoanalysis. 3. Psychotherapist and patient.
I. Title.

RC506.B843 2005
616.89'17—dc22   2004029362

    ISBN-13: 978-0-7657-0382-8 (cloth : alk. paper)
    ISBN-10: 0-7657-0382-3 (cloth : alk. paper)
    ISBN-13: 978-0-7657-0383-5 (pbk. : alk. paper)
    ISBN-10: 0-7657-0383-1 (pbk. : alk. paper)

Printed in the United States of America

⊗™ The paper used in this publication meets the minimum requirements of American
National Standard for Information Sciences—Permanence of Paper for Printed Library
Materials, ANSI/NISO Z39.48-1992.

To Gloria Watson-Kerr and Barry Kaplowitz, for their
devotion to my parents and their friendship to me

Instead of technique, we propose that psychoanalysis is a kind of practice in the Aristotelian sense. . . . Unlike technique, practice is always oriented to the particular. Practice embodies an attitude of inquiry, deliberation and discovery. It eschews rules, but loves questions—questions about what is wise to do with this person, at this time, for this reason.

—Orange, Atwood, and Stolorow (1997)

Contents

Foreword

Both words in the title of this book are rich with meanings. "Intersubjectively" refers in this book primarily to the intersubjective systems theory on which several contributors, especially including Robert Stolorow, George Atwood, Bernard Brandchaft, and I have been at work for many years. (Recent contributors include William Coburn, Maxwell Sucharov, and the author of this book.) Added to the central claim that all psychological life emerges from the interplay of two or more worlds of experience, our work involves an ever-developing interest in European phenomenology and hermeneutics; a fallibilistic epistemology of perspectival realism; interests in complexity, context, and organic systems; and, above all, a relentless determination to understand our patients' worlds of experience as they are lived together with our own. Clinically speaking, this means we engage with our patients in searching for the emotional convictions organizing the patient's experience and our own, especially those that keep them and us suffering and rigidified. We also watch constantly to keep ourselves from imposing our "realistic" preconceptions about facts and values on our patients, in part because we are skeptics about the existence of interpretation-free facts, and in part because we believe that a know-it-all attitude closes down the process of understanding and psychological transformation.

Second, this title uses the word "practice" to describe clinical work. Years ago, I wrote that the concept of practice could well replace that of technique in psychoanalysis. Aristotle's *phronesis* is the practical reasoning that searches for the right thing to do at the right time for the right reason. It resembles Winnicott's "good-enough" kind of relational rightness, the attunement and reattunement of the developmentalists, and the artistry that goes beyond the perfect technique of the craftsman. The philosopher Gadamer makes it clear why practice as phronesis captures so well the spirit of inter-subjectively oriented psychoanalysis and psychotherapy:

> It appears in the fact of concern, not about myself, but about the other person. Thus it is a mode of moral judgment. . . . The question here, then, is not of a general kind of knowledge, but of its specification at a particular moment. This knowledge also is not in any sense technical knowledge or the application of such. . . . The person with understanding does not know and judge as one who stands apart and unaffected; but rather, as one united by a specific bond with the other, he thinks with the other and undergoes the situation with him (Gadamer 1975/1991, p. 288).

Choosing, then, to call our work "practicing," as Peter Buirski and his collaborators do in this book, characterizes our work as a dialogic and relational search for understanding. Each chapter in this book extends the possibilities for living intersubjective systems theory in our daily practice.

Often doubters ask, "But how can such a practice be taught and learned? Surely it is better for beginners to learn a few rules and rely on these." My own answer is both Gadamerian and Aristotelian: practice embodies an attitude of inquiry, deliberation, and discovery. It eschews rules, but loves questions—questions about what is wise to do with this persona, at this time, for this reason, and so on. Such wisdom can be learned, never on the basis of rules, but from the person who lives wisely. So-called training, in my view, is a form of apprenticeship. The wisdom embodied in this book is an opportunity for continued apprenticeship to those whose work has taught them a certain practical wisdom.

It is a major honor to be asked to introduce this book to its readers, because the author has done my collaborators and me such an enormous honor by his engagement with our work. I hope the readers will have as much pleasure in the reading and consideration of these pages as I do in entrusting this book to their practicing hands.

Donna Orange

Acknowledgments

This book was originally conceived as a sequel to *Making Sense Together: The Intersubjective Approach to Psychotherapy* that I wrote with Pamela Haglund, PsyD. Unfortunately for *Practicing Intersubjectively*, when the time came to begin working on this new book, Pam no longer had the time to devote to this project. Her candidacy at the Denver Institute for Psychoanalysis was keeping her far too busy. Fortunately, she has graciously made time to review the other chapters that we had previously written together and those chapters that I wrote or coauthored with others. Thus, in many ways, her stamp is clearly on this book.

I want to thank those colleagues and friends with whom I have discussed these ideas and whose insights, encouragement, and support have been enlightening and sustaining: Elliot Adler, PhD, Harold Cook, PhD, Shelley Doctors, PhD, Abe Fenster, PhD, David Hurst, MD, Michael Karson, PhD, Fernand Lubuguin, PhD, Alan Melowsky, PhD, Lavita Nadkarni, PhD, Lynn Rosdal, PsyD, Robert Shapiro, PhD, Ruth Shapiro, PhD, and Jonathan Shedler, PhD. I am also grateful to other colleagues who have given helpful feedback to individual chapters: David L. Becker, PsyD, and Carol R. Bowman, PsyD, gave input to chapter 6; Martha Ryan, PsyD, in addition to coauthoring chapter 6, made valuable contributions to chapter 5; and Fred Wright, PhD, made significant contributions to chapter 3. I am especially indebted to Donna Orange, PhD, PsyD, and Robert Stolorow, PhD, for their friendship and support.

Many students and supervisees at the Graduate School of Professional Psychology at the University of Denver have contributed to the development of my thinking and practice. Their probing questions and astute observations have broadened and enriched the ideas that have found their way into this book. Their intelligence and critical thinking challenged me to be more articulate. Special thanks go to Samual Adams, Melissa Baker, Katy Barrs, Jessica Bloomfield, Christina Clancy, William Clancy, Rae Sandler, Duncan Seawell, Shawn Smith, Preeti Vidwans, and Christina Walker. The students in my Intersubjective Systems Theory course, Spring 2004, were especially constructive, reading and commenting on several chapters, and I thank them collectively. Finally, Stacie Barnes and Emily Eschbacher provided invaluable assistance tracking down references, copying articles, transcribing videotapes, and doing general editorial consulting. Emily read the book aloud to me, and together we were able to identify and clarify awkward sentences and unclear expressions.

I am grateful to Tracie Kruse for her competence, tact, good judgment, and friendship. She always managed to keep the ship on course when I was preoccupied with projects like this one.

I also want to express my deepest appreciation to those people who, over the years, have been open to engaging in a therapy relationship with me.

Finally, to my family: my wife, Cathy Krown Buirski, MSW, has been a loving friend, companion, and colleague with whom I have shared so much, both intellectually and emotionally; and my son Max and my daughter Diana have been supportive, encouraging, and affirming with their interest in and understanding of these ideas.

Introduction

While the term "intersubjectivity" is used differently by various relational theorists, my thinking about Intersubjective Systems Theory draws heavily on the work of Stolorow, Atwood, and Orange. My desire to write this book grew out of what was left unsaid in *Making Sense Together: The Intersubjective Approach to Psychotherapy* that I wrote with Pamela Haglund. In *Practicing Intersubjectively*, I try to explicate and elucidate the way an intersubjective systems sensibility can inform and enrich the broad range of clinical practice.

Students and colleagues often ask what an intersubjectivist would say in a particular clinical exchange. This is a tricky question because it seems to address issues of technique and focus on contents. First, let me say that I am not representing myself as the "voice" of intersubjective systems theory. While many people may be informed by the intersubjective systems sensibility, everyone makes sense of it and practices in their own ways. There is no uniform body of technique that defines our perspective. If we agree on anything, it is that each treatment is unique and must be invented afresh by the participants. In this regard, intersubjective systems theory views each treatment as exquisitely context sensitive. This means that the person who comes for therapy would present differently to different therapists, and the two of them would construct different processes. Therapists themselves are not interchangeable, and the intersubjective field that the two participants create together would be quite different from the field created by any other pair. An articulation that might have felt right yesterday might not feel right today. As we say, "It depends."

Second, what I, as the therapist, hear when the other is speaking is very much delimited by my view of the way people develop and the range of experiences that can disrupt or facilitate that development. That is, in the clinical moment, what I hear the other saying is constrained by my theory of mind, my clinical experience, and the current state of my life. My first psychoanalytic language was Freudian theory. I still can speak it, but I am losing my fluency. Now I tend to experience it as an interference or distraction, like static on the radio. If the person I'm talking with says, "I felt attracted to a woman much taller than me," I try not to get distracted by focusing on the Oedipal derivative (mother was obviously taller), if I hear it at all. The meaning of the "taller woman" might indeed turn out to have Oedipal components; intersubjective systems theory doesn't exclude any meanings, even those that are consistent with the expectations of other theories of mental functioning. We are devoted to promoting the unfolding and illumination of personal meanings, without personal investment in where our journey will take us.

This may sound like something contemporary Freudians would agree with, and at this point I do hear the voices of my friends objecting that I am creating differences where none exist. However, it is a much more complex subject than this may sound. While all experienced analysts would take as self-evident that we must explore the meaning something has for the other, the essence of the intersubjective perspective is that we cannot easily de-center ourselves from our worldviews. This point comes up throughout the book. It would be a bit like saying, "I don't hold prejudiced beliefs consciously or unconsciously." If something is unconscious, then, by definition, we cannot know it. Those of us whose training has been in models of the mind that emphasize universals, like the Oedipus complex, Mahler's separation-individuation stages, or Kleinian positions for example, listen and hear differently than those who haven't been steeped in these traditions. Our personal worlds of experience and the meanings we make cannot help but be colored by our theoretical and experiential worldviews. I have tried to illustrate this point in chapters 2 and 3, where the therapist's theory of mind impacts the therapeutic encounter in powerful ways.

This raises a third point: that what a therapist working from an intersubjective systems sensibility might say in a particular clinical interchange may not sound very different from what any experienced therapist might say. Intersubjective systems theory emphasizes the mutual and reciprocal influence of two subjectivities on each other, but privileges the other's subjectivity. As Orange (1995) has observed, psychotherapy involves two people trying to make sense of one. Therefore, I try to articulate my grasp of the other's subjective world of experience, which is what I believe most good therapists, regardless of theory, do most of the time. Perhaps the difference lies in the inverse: what distinguishes the therapist working from the intersubjective systems perspective from therapists working from other orientations is to be found more in what they do not do or say than in what they actually do or say. For example, we try to avoid taking an objectivist stance, assuming that we are privy to some greater authority or knowledge than the other. And we avoid pathologizing, which is revealed by a focus on the person's maladaptive behaviors or motives, like his masochism. Instead, we wonder about how the person's striving for health might be obscured by behaviors or motives that appear self-defeating.

Fourth, while those practicing intersubjectively believe in the importance of making unconscious organizations of experience more accessible to consciousness, we focus as much on the reparative quality of our relationship with those with whom we work. While the notion of a curative emotional experience has been discredited in the traditional literature, I remain convinced that one of the important promoters of growth and health is the inverse of what disrupted it in the first place: the quality of emotional relating between people who are important to each other. If the consistent misattunement of the early caregivers plays a large role in the child's emotional impairment, then repair must necessarily involve a new and improved attuned relationship.

This book is concerned with describing how the intersubjective systems perspective informs, shapes, and guides the psychotherapeutic process. One of the great strengths of the intersubjective systems perspective, largely because it is a contextual and systems perspective, is that practicing intersubjectively enriches the work done in diverse clinical contexts. To illustrate the broad applicability of the intersubjective systems perspective, I have applied it in traditional and nontraditional contexts. For example, I have included chapters on working with people from diverse multicultural backgrounds, people with prejudiced attitudes, and people suffering from trauma. In addition, I have retrospectively applied the intersubjective systems perspective to one of the most famous cases in the psychoanalytic literature, Freud's case of the Wolf Man.

I have tried to develop these ideas using as little technical jargon as possible. However, each theory speaks in its own specialized language and requires its own vocabulary. Therefore, becoming fluent in the language of intersubjective systems theory requires adjusting one's ear to new terms and concepts. Sometimes familiar terms and concepts are used in new ways with new meanings. This is an unfortunate source of confusion, and, where possible, I have tried to use nontechnical words to clarify different meanings.

Finally, the reader will notice that I have made an effort, sometimes awkward sounding, to avoid the use of the term "patient" to refer to the person who engages in self-exploration with the therapist. Liz Shane (2001), in her review of *Making Sense Together*, stressed this contradiction and I appreciate her point. While the Latin root of "patient" refers to one who suffers, contemporary usage derives from the medical model and signifies the person that the physician heals. One person is doing something to another, not two people co-constructing experience. "Patient" suggests the very one-person, objectivist, hierarchical model of relationship that the intersubjective systems perspective abhors. "Client" is no better a term, with its implications of a business relationship. Even though psychotherapists charge for their time and expertise, it is not a business relationship. It is the most personal and intimate of encounters, from which both will emerge enriched. When the term "patient" does occur in the text, it is used in the context of one-person, hierarchical, isolated mind thinking.

The book contains eight chapters, some of which I have coauthored with others and some I have written alone. Some chapters have appeared separately, in modified form, and others appear here for the first time.

Chapter 1, 'There's No Such Thing as a Patient,' coauthored with Pamela Haglund, PsyD, begins with an overview of the theory of intersubjectivity. Haglund and I introduce the language of intersubjectivity and try to give a clear description of the fundamental concepts. Theory necessarily informs practice, and chapter 1 provides the framework for later chapters on practice. In this chapter, we assert that a contextual view of mind cannot be reconciled with any concepts referring to isolated mental contents or processes. We challenge the position that it is possible for clinicians to embrace both a relational, contextualist, two-or-more person view of psychology and a perspective that views defenses, fantasies, or any observable clinical material as originating solely within the mind of the individual. Rather, we illustrate that whatever emerges clinically can be understood only as a phenomenon of the field consisting of both participants. A version of this chapter will appear in *Psychoanalysis and Psychotherapy*, Spring 2005.

Chapter 2, "Innocent Analyst or Implicated Analyst," makes use of a previously published case report by Martin Silverman (1987) to illustrate how the therapist's theory of mind shapes the therapeutic encounter. Through an examination of clinical material generated in four consecutive sessions, the differences between the structural theory approach of Silverman and an intersubjective systems sensibility becomes evident. In this chapter, I try to show how the theory of the analyst leads to clinical choices that profoundly influence and shape the psychoanalytic process.

Chapter 3, "Two Approaches to Psychotherapy," further illustrates the distinctive treatment implications that the contemporary Freudian and intersubjective systems approaches have on the unfolding therapy dialogue. In this chapter I present the transcript of an initial interview that grew out of a demonstration of the psychodynamic approach conducted at John Jay College of Criminal Justice. To avoid the ethical concerns raised by doing a public demonstration with someone seeking psychological help, an actor was enlisted to develop and improvise the person of Mr. G. I began this interview from the stance informed by my understanding of contemporary structural theory, focusing on promoting insight and understanding. Midway through the interview, I got the strong impression that I was fostering defensiveness and narcissistic injury in Mr. G, so I consciously and deliberately switched stances to an approach informed by intersubjective sensibility. This interview provides an opportunity to contrast the differential impact that these two approaches have on the unfolding process.

Chapter 4, "Colliding Worlds of Experience," examines the complications that arise when people, informed by the isolated mind perspective pervading the common cultural wisdom, encounter therapists working from the intersubjective systems perspective. I distinguish between resistance, disjunction, confrontation, and collision and offer a new look at the transformative potential that grows out of the collision between the divergent worldviews held by the members of the therapy dyad.

Chapter 5, "An Intersubjective Systems Perspective on Multicultural Treatment," coauthored with Michelle Doft, PsyD, describes how an intersubjective systems sensibility lends itself to working with people from ethnic, racial, and cultural backgrounds that are different from that of the therapist. With its commitment to the empathic/introspective stance and attunement to the subjective experience of the other, the intersubjective field becomes enriched by multicultural experience. A version of this chapter is in press at the journal *Psychoanalysis and Contemporary Thought* and is presented here with permission.

Chapter 6, "Prejudice as a Function of Self-Organization," coauthored with Martha Kendall Ryan, PsyD, reviews the traditional psychoanalytic theories of the development and maintenance of prejudiced attitudes and affects. To this body of understanding we offer an intersubjectively informed self psychological perspective. We describe the treatment of Sandy, a woman who presented with extreme expressions of prejudice, to illustrate how this perspective provides a framework for understanding the narcissistic roots of her prejudice and a therapeutic stance for promoting the transformation of her prejudiced attitudes and affects. From this perspective, prejudice is understood, not as the displacement or projection of aggression, but as an expression of a vulnerable, fragmentation-prone self-organization struggling to overcome a traumatic developmental history. A version of this essay was published in *Psychoanalytic Psychology*, 2001 (18), 21–36, and is presented here with permission.

In chapter 7, "Bearing Witness to Trauma from an Intersubjective Systems Perspective: A Case Study," coauthored with Erin Shrago, PsyD, we show how an intersubjective systems perspective can be applied to treating a victim of a traumatic experience. We address the controversial topic of therapist self-disclosure by examining some of the various meanings that American relational theory and self-psychology have derived from it. We attempt to integrate the various perspectives on self-disclosure by focusing on the selfobject function of bearing witness. Through a focus on the therapist's bearing witness to the victim's suffering, a field is created in which both participants benefited.

Chapter 8, "The Wolf Man's Subjective Experience of His Treatment with Freud," is coauthored with Pamela Haglund, PsyD. In the preceding chapters, my collaborators and I have examined the application of intersubjective systems theory to a wide range of situations encountered in clinical practice. Now I would like to apply the lens of intersubjective systems theory to one of the most famous cases in the psychoanalytic literature—Freud's case of the Wolf Man. We know little about how Freud actually conducted a treatment. However, from Serge Pankejeff's (the Wolf Man) subjective experience of his treatment with Freud, as reported in his memoirs and published interviews, we gain a unique perspective on the impact of the contextual factors influencing Freud's approach to this treatment. The purpose of this chapter is to extract from Pankejeff's subjective experience of Freud those aspects of their work together that were most memorable and meaningful for the patient. Freud's work with Pankejeff has been severely criticized for breaching his own technical recommendations. However, we suggest that, in fact, it was these very controversial intersubjectively constructed interventions that were experienced by Pankejeff as most therapeutic. Furthermore, we propose that Freud extracted from Pankejeff's symptoms those features that confirmed his theory of infantile sexuality and, in so doing, overlooked Pankejeff's grief and depression. A version of this essay was published in *Psychoanalytic Psychology*, 1998 (15), 49–62, and is presented here with permission.

Chapter One

"There's No Such Thing as a Patient"[1]

Coauthored with
Pamela Haglund, PsyD

Psychoanalysis is a living discipline. Its body of theoretical and clinical knowledge has been evolving rapidly, nowhere more noticeably than in its encounter with the relational perspective. In many ways, the contemporary trajectory of psychoanalytic thought can be understood as a struggle to reconcile the intrapsychic, one-person, objectivist perspective with the intersubjective, contextual perspective of the relational turn.

There have been various approaches to reconciling the Freudian and relational traditions. One attempt, represented by Goretti (2001), is to argue that there is nothing new in relational thinking that can't be found in Freud's own writings. She makes the case that Freud, from the beginning, incorporated many relational ideas into his thinking. For example, she points to Freud's discussion of the Dora case (1953 [1905a]) as evidence of Freud's sensitivity to the impact of the analyst on the analytic process. The point being advanced is that, in essence, the relational perspective offers little that is new or different from what was already implicit in Freudian theory.

Another approach acknowledges the neglect of relational influences in traditional theory and technique and strives to integrate some relational ideas into clinical practice. Certainly notions like the therapeutic alliance (Zetzel 1956), the working alliance (Greenson 1967), and the importance of the real relationship (Loewald 1960) have been in our literature for some time, pointing to the importance of addressing the relationship between patient and analyst.

Today, there is an excitement in the air and a lively debate in the literature over, not the merits of relational constructs, but the extent to which relational thinking should either serve as an important addition to contemporary Freudian psychoanalytic thinking or supplant it entirely on the grounds that

1

the relational perspective is fundamentally incompatible and irreconcilable with traditional theory. The central disagreement is that while there is merit to the new ideas offered by modern relational theories like intersubjective systems theory, the old ideas still have value and clinical utility. Why discard such useful constructs as the id, ego, superego, transference, compulsions to repeat, compromise formations, and the like when modern Freudians have been successfully melding these constructs with a more relational way of engaging with patients? This perspective takes an integrative approach to the problem: Why not "both/and" instead of "either/or"? The argument is that intersubjective systems theory should not throw the baby out with the bathwater.

There are numerous voices on the "both/and" side. Wasserman (1999) advocates what he calls "an 'integrative stance,' which attempts to integrate elements of one- and two-person psychologies while retaining interpretation as primary in bringing about change" (p. 449). More recently, Pray (2002) takes the position that we could maintain a unified theoretical stance, were it not for "our natural inclination against holding competing or incompatible perspectives" (p. 253). Shapiro (2002) seeks to bypass the problems posed by a two-person psychology by examining the conversational rules that govern monologue and dialogue.

Then there is the perspective of many relational thinkers who have discussed and wrestled with the substantial and perhaps irreconcilable differences between theories of mental functioning that privilege an intrapsychic view of human motivation and those that view mind and motive as relational constructs. As Greenberg and Mitchell (1983) have stated:

> The manner in which one understands the basic nature of human experience and the fundamental motives of human behavior informs one's understanding of the nature of the psychoanalytic situation and analytic process. The drive model and the relational model embody fundamentally different visions of human nature, and the theories of technique which have developed from them are similarly divergent in their basic premises (p. 388).

Mitchell (1988) went on to observe that, "Either interaction is viewed in the context of the expression of preformed forces or pressures, or mental content is viewed as expressed and shaped in the context of the establishment and maintenance of connections with others" (p. 5). In this vein, Modell (1984) concluded that the two models belong to "two different conceptual realms . . . two apparently irreconcilable contexts" (pp. 257–58).

While intersubjective systems theory is certainly relational, it differs in important ways from Mitchell's (1988) relational theory and other theories that describe themselves in terms of intersubjectivity, like Daniel Stern

(1985), Benjamin (1995a, 1995b), and Ogden (1994). Intersubjective systems theory is most fundamentally a radically contextual perspective and not a theory of mental contents and structures. According to Stolorow, Orange, and Atwood (2001), "an intersubjective field—any system constituted by interacting experiential worlds—is neither a mode of experiencing nor a sharing of experience. It is the contextual precondition for having any experience at all" (p. 474).

A large part of the gulf that separates these various theoretical camps is philosophical and linguistic. Contemporary Freudian thinkers have their philosophical roots in the worldview associated with the philosophy of Descartes. To some extent, this is also true of many relational theories (Stolorow, Orange, and Atwood 2001). In contrast, the intersubjective systems perspective has its philosophical roots in the hermeneutic tradition and the existential–phenomenological movement (Atwood and Stolorow 1984).

The intersubjective systems perspective holds that all human experience and the meanings made of it are formed, shaped, and embedded in worlds of personal experience. This fundamental idea has found important empirical support from the infant development research, like the work of Beebe and Lachmann (2002). While the notion of making theory and treatment "experience near" has been discussed in the psychoanalytic literature for a while, before recent developments in infant research, it has been beyond our knowledge to describe our theories as being "research near." However, its compatibility with developmental research findings enhances the philosophical underpinnings of intersubjective systems theory.

Beebe and Lachmann (2002), for example, focus on the infant research literature that analyzes the face-to-face interactions of mother and infant on a second-by-second basis. Drawing on the nonlinear dynamic systems perspective of Thelen and Smith (1994), Beebe and Lachmann locate psychoanalysis and adult treatment within a systems view of interaction that is compatible with some current infant and adult research. From their analysis of this research, mind is seen as relationally constructed, and "interactiveness" becomes central to psychoanalytic thinking. According to Beebe and Lachmann (2002), "Rather than conceiving of self as interacting with other, we conceptualize an ongoing co-construction of processes of self- and interactive regulation. Interactiveness is emergent, in a constant process of potential reorganization" (p. 224).

Intersubjective systems theory is an overarching perspective. As articulated by its leading proponents, Stolorow, Atwood, Brandchaft, and Orange, it is a "metatheory" and not a specific theory of mental contents and structures or metapsychology, nor is it a developmental stage (Stern 1985) or developmental achievement (Benjamin 1990). Intersubjective systems theory is a field or systems theory that has, as its central concern, the impact of contextual and systemic factors on personal worlds of experience. According to Stolorow and Atwood (1992), "the concept of an intersubjective system brings to focus *both* the individual's world of inner experience *and* its embeddedness with other such worlds in a continual flow of reciprocal mutual influence" (p. 18). Intersubjective systems theory views human development, in its healthy and pathological forms, as taking shape in a relational context. The relational context, the intersubjective field, is the medium in which personality in all its complexity takes form and continues to be manifested. Relatedness plays a constitutive role in the organization of worlds of personal experience.

Mind, as understood by current developmental research, is a relational construction. As we have discussed previously, there is no subjectivity without intersubjectivity and there can be no intersubjectivity without subjectivity (Buirski and Haglund 2001). That is, subjective worlds of personal experience are inextricably embedded in intersubjective systems. When viewed from a systems or contextual perspective, distinctions, like those between one-person and two-person psychologies, are revealed as too limited because worlds of personal experience encompass more than just the two people involved.

Let us play with a baseball analogy. Home runs are co-constructed by the different contributions of both batter and pitcher. When Barry Bonds set the all-time single-season home run record in 2001, he faced thousands of pitched balls but hit only seventy-three home runs. Why so few? Some pitches were so far out of the strike zone that they could not be hit or hit with power. Some pitches were too fast, too slow, too well placed, or curved unexpectedly. Despite the fact that so few pitches were turned into home runs, Bonds hit more in one season than any other batter in the history of the game. Clearly, Bonds brought something unique to the plate with him—his timing, hand-eye coordination, strength, experience—that made him more able than others to hit home runs. Against some pitchers, Bonds hit many home runs; against others, he hit few or none. No doubt the pitchers were bringing some of their own talents and abilities to the encounter. Whether a given pitch resulted in a home run depended on both what the pitcher brought and what the batter brought to their encounter. But, whether a particular swing culminated in a home run was influenced by factors other than what batter and pitcher contributed. Cold weather, hot weather, rain, or wind direction and speed were contextual factors that contributed to the construction of the hit or miss. So, too, were the size and shape of the ballpark and the altitude and thin air of parks like Coors Field. We could go on identifying numerous other contextual contributors to the end result. Clearly, it would be inaccurate to say that the home run was co-constructed when so many factors, in addition to hitter and pitcher, contribute to the end result. It would be more accurate to say that home runs are contextually constructed. The home run analogy can be pushed further.[2] When a hitter comes to bat against a particular pitcher, he brings along memories of his prior experience with that pitcher, and vice versa. These memories modify his expectations of how he will be pitched to. Similarly, the pitcher knows what worked or didn't in previous encounters and modifies his selection of pitches accordingly. In other words, both hitter and pitcher are engaged in self- and interactive regulation; both are influencing and being influenced by the other. We can borrow Winnicott's (1965) observation and metaphorically say that there is no such thing as Barry Bonds. There is only Bonds in this at bat against this pitcher in this point in this game in this stadium and so on.

This view of the formation of human experience and the personal meanings made of it has profound implications for psychoanalytic theory and practice. And it is at this point that we are forced to choose. Do we maintain our allegiance to traditional metapsychological formulations despite their incompatibility with current philosophical and research-based conceptions of mental functioning or do we revise or discard them in order for psychoanalysis to fit better with more modern understandings?

When we are cautioned by contemporary Freudians not to throw the baby out with the bathwater, it raises the question of what exactly is "the baby" that we should preserve. When we try to pare down to its bare essentials the nature of this necessary "baby," we think that it refers to constructs and presumed mental contents that have proved useful in practice. These constructs and contents seem to be tied to a set of metapsychological concepts that are thought to account for human motivation. We are referring to such metapsychological constructs as an intrapsychic realm thought to exist within the mind of the individual; structural theory concerning the interplay of id, ego, and superego structures within that realm; the economic point of view concerning the relative strength of these structures; the dynamic interplay of these structures; and the adaptive point of view that there is an objectively knowable reality that the isolated mind of the individual must contend with.

Criticism of these traditional metapsychological constructs, the psychoanalytic "baby" if you will, is not new. For instance, in the 1970s, psychoanalysts like Merton Gill (1976) and George Klein (1976) attempted to rid clinical practice of its ties to metapsychology on the grounds that metapsychology derives from a flawed understanding of human motivation and functioning. According to Stolorow (1978),

Metapsychology deals with the material substrate of subjective experience and is thus couched in the natural science framework of impersonal structures, forces and energies which are presumed to actually "exist" as entities or events in the realm of objective reality. . . . Metapsychology is concerned with "how" questions and seeks answers in terms of the "non-experiential realm" of impersonal mechanisms and causes (p. 313).

And most recently, Charles Brenner (2002) has advocated discarding structural theory entirely. According to Brenner, "present knowledge of mental conflict and compromise formation renders invalid the widely accepted theory of mind as functionally separable structures called id, ego, and superego" (p. 397). For Brenner, then, the indispensable psychoanalytic "baby" can be reduced to mental conflict and compromise formation.

As we mentioned previously, traditional psychoanalytic metapsychology has its philosophical roots in a worldview articulated by Descartes. This historical psychoanalytic worldview, described by its adherence to Cartesian thinking, needs to be distinguished from perspectives, such as the intersubjective systems view, that focus on a post-Cartesian contextualism. Cavell (1993), Orange (2001), and Stolorow, Atwood, and Orange (2002) have eloquently articulated some of the implications of this Cartesian view of mind and contrasted it with a post-Cartesian view that is much more compatible with contemporary developmental research. According to Stolorow, Atwood, and Orange (2002),

> The assumptions of traditional psychoanalysis have been pervaded by the Cartesian doctrine of the isolated mind. This doctrine bifurcates the subjective world of the person into outer and inner regions, reifies and absolutizes the resulting separation between the two and pictures the mind as an objective entity that takes its place among other objects, a "thinking thing" that has an inside with contents and looks out on an external world from which it is essentially estranged (pp. 1–2).

Other features of the Cartesian mind that have long been embedded in Western thought are the values of empiricism and positivism, the idea of an external objectively knowable world and the corollary conviction that the analyst possesses a uniquely objective perspective on the experience of the patient. These aspects of the Cartesian mind have been captured by Stolorow and Atwood's (1992) discussion of what they term "the myth of the isolated mind" (p. 7).

The essence of the myth of the isolated mind is that the human mind is a self-contained and self-sufficient internal structure that is independent of an objectively knowable external world. When we contrast psychic reality with external reality, as if the two were separable and distinct regions, we are engaging in just this kind of isolated-mind thinking. Traditionally, the analyst was thought to have a unique, objective perspective on the reality of the patient's experience, while the patient had a distorted view of himself and the outside world. While we do not question that physics and chemistry can tell us a great deal about the outside world, the post-Cartesian perspective asserts that psychoanalysis cannot tell us anything objective about the outside world, separate from our personal experience of that world. As research on the unreliability of eyewitness testimony has revealed, the eye of the beholder is an interpretive lens, not a scientific measuring device (Brandon and Davies 1973; Ellison and Buckhout 1981).

For example, if a woman complains to her therapist that her husband verbally intimidates her, there is no way for our psychoanalytic method to verify or dispute the "objective reality" of this complaint. Even if in the transference, the woman feels that the therapist also verbally intimidates her, we cannot dispute the subjective nature of her experience of feeling verbally intimidated. The therapist might think privately that he has not been verbally intimidating, but rather, that the woman is overly sensitive. Of course, if the therapist were to interpret this, he would be guilty of imposing his version of "reality" on the woman and thereby risk confirming the woman's subjective experience that the therapist has indeed been verbally intimidating. In other words, the appearance in the transference of a similar relational configuration in no way invalidates or disconfirms the woman's subjective experience that her husband has been verbally abusive, nor does it confirm the therapist's position that the woman "is" overly sensitive. What this example does highlight is the fallible nature of the therapist's authority and illustrates the impossibility of finding either objective truth or pathological distortion through psychoanalytic means.

Another example of isolated-mind thinking is evident in the Axis II designations of the DSM-IV-TR (American Psychiatric Association 2000). If he meets the specified criteria, a man may be labeled with a personality disorder, as in, "He is a borderline." Such diagnoses or labels treat the individual as separate and distinct from the experiential world in which he is immersed. "Borderline" is viewed as an immutable state, a condition that exists in isolation, as if the individual's way of relating was unaffected by the relational context in which he finds himself. From the post-Cartesian, contextualist perspective, "borderline" is not a fixed state or a condition like measles—if I have it with John today, I will also show it with Mary. Rather, it is a range of behaviors that are elicited in certain contexts and not others—if I manifest these behaviors with John today, I might or might not enact them with him tomorrow or with Mary anytime. This perspective clearly diverges from one that assumes personality traits are an enduring and inseparable part of the whole person, like his or her head.

The influence of isolated-mind notions can be seen in "psychoanalytic doctrines that focus exclusively on processes occurring within the individual person . . . (including), for example, Freud's vision of the mind as an impersonal machine that processes endogenous drive energies, ego psychology's autonomously self-regulating ego, and Kohut's pristine self with its preprogrammed inner design" (Orange, Atwood, and Stolorow 1997, p. 42). If you cannot separate the external material world from the inner world of experience, then it doesn't make much sense to theorize about such things as the ego being formed out of the conflict between inner experience and external reality, as ego psychology proposes, or that external objects become internalized in an inner realm, as object relations theories propose.

Let us examine the concept of the intrapsychic structure of mind, since it is a crucial aspect of the psychoanalytic "baby." The concept of the intrapsychic can be traced back to the earliest foundations of Freud's psychoanalytic theorizing. The defining psychoanalytic moment occurred when Freud revised his earlier notion that neurosis resulted from a real, external sexual trauma experienced in relationship to an important other. His (Freud 1953 [1905b]) great psychoanalytic insight was that what was recalled by his people in analysis was not always the memory of real traumatic events inflicted by an external other, as he had thought earlier (1895), but often was the memory of an internally generated fantasy. This insight took the formation of psychopathology out of the realm of the interpersonal and placed it squarely in the intrapsychic world of the individual isolated mind. In some cases, for Freud, the child was traumatizing itself with its own internally generated fantasies and wishes. The focus of psychoanalytic treatment became the internal world of endogenous drives, fantasies, and wishes, the defenses against the knowledge of these fantasies and wishes and the compromise formations that resulted from the inherent conflict between wishes and defenses.

Since the focus of traditional psychoanalysis has been on the intrapsychic realm, surely psychoanalysis could be said to have made subjectivity its special province. We suggest that the notion of mind as an intrapsychic structure is very different from considerations of subjectivity or personal worlds of experience. The intrapsychic is concerned with structure and content. A notion of intrapsychic mind implies that the mind of the individual is a self-contained thing that exists in isolation from the many contexts in which it is experienced. Endogenous sources of stimulation, whether from biologically based drives or the wishes derived from them, are seen as inevitably in conflict with internalized restraints and the demands of the objectively known, external "real" world.

Subjectivity refers to personal worlds of experience in contrast to internalized structures and contents. Personal worlds of experience do not presuppose any universal contents, like the Oedipus complex or paranoid/schizoid or depressive positions. The idea of universal mental contents is completely at odds with the notion that experience is contextually constituted; that personal meanings are continually constructed and reconstructed within a relational context and are not generated solely from within one of the players.

Too often in psychoanalytic theorizing, the subject has been understood as an isolated mind interacting with its object, another isolated mind. But subject, as a thing, is very different from subjectivity, which refers to phenomenological worlds of experience. Our point is that the person as the object of scrutiny, as in a one-person psychology, cannot be understood separately from the intersubjective contexts in which subjective worlds of experience are constituted and embedded. However, what have been referred to as two-person psychologies are often nothing more than two isolated minds interacting with each other. As long as we are dealing with isolated minds, we neglect the constitutive nature of our embeddedness in personal worlds of experience.

There is an important difference between rejecting the idea of universal mental contents and denying that any particular personal meaning might be made within some intersubjective systems. Experience may get organized into any conceivable pattern of meaning, like the Oedipus complex. We emphasize that each pattern is uniquely constituted within a particular intersubjective field and that no universal patterns are generated regardless of seemingly similar contexts. For example, each child in a family is different, not just because 50 percent of their genetic makeup is not shared, but because, even though they live in the same house with the same parents, their personal worlds of experience and the meanings they make of them are unique to the individual. Like any self-fulfilling prophecy, the expectation of finding any specific organization of experience will influence and shape what is created. Isolated-mind notions, far from revealing hidden meanings, often instigate their own construction. If, for example, one believes that the Oedipus complex is universal, one will surely find it or derivatives of it, or defenses against it, or symbolic representations of it wherever one looks.

Another problem with the notion of the intrapsychic structure of mind is that it perpetuates the Cartesian distinction between inner and outer reality. This raises the question of who is to be the arbiter of what is reality. Traditionally, the analyst was presumed to be an authority on the nature of the analysand's inner reality and how this inner reality denies, distorts, or is unaware of some objectively knowable external reality. From the contextualist perspective, inner and outer realities are metaphors that cannot be objectively known by psychoanalytic methods.

Rejecting the notion of the intrapsychic structure of mind does not necessitate a rejection of the notion of the unconscious process. The intersubjective systems perspective is often misunderstood as being strictly concerned with conscious experience. If this were the case, then it would certainly be superficial and lack depth. But the notion of subjective worlds of experience does not preclude aspects of experiential worlds that may not be readily accessible to conscious examination or exploration. We agree that people often avoid knowing or disavow aspects of their emotional experience that would be disturbing or frightening. But we do not turn to spatial metaphors, like "the unconscious" or dynamic forces, like repression, to capture this aspect of subjective experience. From the perspective of contextualized experiential worlds, unconsciousness refers to the realms of experience that have been limited by the responsiveness of the surround.

> Forming and evolving within a nexus of living systems, experiential worlds and their horizons are recognized as being exquisitely context-sensitive and context-dependent. The horizons of awareness are thus fluid and ever-shifting, products both of the person's unique intersubjective history and of what is or is not allowed to be known within the intersubjective fields that constitute his or her current living (Stolorow, Atwood, and Orange 2002, p. 47).

Other metapsychological constructs suffer from many of the same Cartesian problems that plague the concept of intrapsychic structure. Freud's view of the mind as a mental machine that requires energy to do work is a particular Cartesian metaphor that derives from the science of physics. The mental machine is the isolated mind and its energy is endogenously generated. Psychological dynamics refer to the interplay of mental structures of differing energic strengths. Psychological conflict occurs between structures of different energic strength interacting, like wishes and defenses, all occurring within an isolated mind, disconnected from and indifferent to its relational contexts.

Most contemporary analysts claim to reject some but not all metapsychological constructs. Often, however, metapsychological perspectives that are rejected on theoretical grounds are still retained in practice, ostensibly for their clinical utility. For instance, many analysts reject traditional Freudian-drive theory, especially as regards the death instinct. However, the notion that aggression builds up within the individual mind and gets expressed as masochism or sadism is regularly invoked to explain behavior even as drive theory is rejected. Some analysts may reject drives in theory, but still believe in what Mitchell (1988) called "the metaphor of the beast" (p. 67), that human nature is propelled by animalistic, antisocial impulses that must be tamed or contained in the process of development.

In another common example, many analysts reject the energy model of drive theory (the economic point of view); however, they nevertheless retain notions like "ego strength," which are steeped in the energy model of quantities or amounts. Similarly, most analysts retain notions like id, ego, and superego, presumably as descriptors of mental functions or activities, but then invoke them clinically as if they were real structures in the mind, like the idea of a rigid or punitive superego.

Let us examine another central metapsychological construct, the dynamic point of view of forces in conflict. The mind in conflict has been central to psychoanalytic thinking going back to Freud's earliest formulations. In the days of the topographic theory, conflict was seen as occurring between the forces of consciousness and the forces of the unconscious. Later, in structural theory, conflict was understood as occurring in the intrapsychic realm between the id, ego, and superego structures of the mind (Freud 1961 [1923]). Here again, we see the separation of a hypothetical internal world from an objectively knowable external reality. Conflict is understood as occurring wholly internally because the external world has presumably been internalized in the form of the superego. This is truly a one-person, isolated-mind perspective that is hard to surrender even for theoretical advocates of two-person, relational, co-constructivist perspectives.

An integral part of the notion of internal mental conflict is the concept of defense. Traditionally, defenses were understood as attempts, on the part of the isolated mind, to ward off internal dangers, that is, dangers arising from the impulse world. Reaction formation, projection, and displacement are examples of the way defenses against internal dangers are thought to distort an accurate view of objective external reality. A few defenses, like denial or dissociation, are presumed to cope with objective external dangers, with similar distorting effects. Then there are defenses, like projective identification, that straddle both internal and external worlds.

Some analysts, who espouse a co-constructivist notion of mental functioning, nevertheless defend projective identification as a clinically useful construct. Projective identification describes a process where the contents of one isolated mind are mysteriously placed into another isolated mind. Invariably, it is the patient whose internal affect state, usually in the form of pernicious aggression, is being put into the innocent analyst, where, like the "Alien," it later bursts forth from inside the analyst to attack the patient. This hypothetical process clearly involves two isolated minds in interaction and not a co-constructed system of reciprocal mutual influence.

These are all isolated-mind notions, whether or not adherents to certain relational perspectives entertain them. As such, they represent flawed metaphors for complex psychological processes that have insinuated themselves into what has become our shared cultural endowment, so much so that they are treated as expressions of ordinary common sense (Stolorow, Atwood, and Orange 2002). Thus, they invariably exert their influence on our clinical work. The problem with isolated-mind notions is that they ignore the contextual foundations for all experience. Isolated-mind constructions are often treated as objectively true expressions of the dynamic workings of the person's mind. The analyst's insights into the analysand's dynamics are then communicated as accurate interpretations about the analysand's mind and motives.

Here is the source of much of our differing perspectives. Traditional and contemporary Freudians see the individual person as the basic unit of study, whereas the intersubjective systems perspective sees the person as embedded in intersecting worlds of personal experience. Intersubjectivity is relational, in the sense of mutual influence and interactive regulation of experience. It is a fundamental, indivisible quality of the field and is not the same as relationship or interpersonal interaction, something that individual minds engage in. This is the crucial point. Analysts advocating Freudian-based theories acknowledge the importance of the therapeutic relationship in their clinical work and focus on developing rapport, working alliances (Greenson 1967), and other connections with their patients. However, promoting rapport, working alliances, and good relationships with people does not make a theory relational. It merely treats relationship as a technique the analyst employs to further the goals of uncovering what is going on in the analysand's isolated mind. From this modern Freudian perspective, treatment is a situation where individual isolated minds come into interaction with each other. To be interested in exploring the depths of a person's mind means that "mind" is a thing or object whose self-contained contents may be studied.

The intersubjective systems perspective rejects all isolated-mind notions because they are incompatible, inconsistent, and ultimately irreconcilable with this view of the contextual nature of personal worlds of experience. The reason the intersubjective systems perspective rejects concepts like reaction formation, projection, displacement, and internalization is that they are founded on flawed, isolated-mind assumptions about human nature and development. Mechanisms like reaction formation, projection, displacement, and internalization presume that one self-contained, isolated mind can move some of its contents to another self-contained, isolated mind or take them in as if they were a foreign body. The problem is that while these constructs may be powerful pictorial metaphors, some theories treat them as if they were real mechanisms. By failing to capture the exquisitely context sensitive and mutually influencing processes at work, these metaphors influence clinical work by shaping how we understand and treat the person.

For example, in the defense of reaction formation, unacceptable feelings or impulses, like love for the analyst, get transformed into hate for that object. This is understood as a strictly intrapsychic process in which the conflict is presumed to concern superego-driven guilt over unacceptable, id-related desires and is not related to any specific qualities of the analyst. Such dynamic understanding then leads to the construction of interpretations about the person's guilt over his or her desires for the analyst. However, such dynamic understandings and interpretations are inadequate since they neglect the systemic or contextual aspects of the analyst's engagement with the analysand that might have stimulated or aroused the analysand's longings, such as the analyst's caring concern, empathic listening, or attuned responding. Unacceptable longings and guilt are presumed to actually exist as powerful, real dynamics operating solely within the analysand's mind. In contrast, from the contextualist perspective, whatever desires the analysand may now be experiencing have been influenced by the context in which they appear and exist neither in the analysand nor in the analyst alone, but in the intersubjective field created by the two.

The intersubjective systems perspective is concerned, not with mind, but with intersecting worlds of personal experience and the personal meanings made of such experience. Treatment is one context where worlds of personal experience intersect. Therefore, the aim of treatment is not the excavation and uncovering of defended-against mental contents, but the unfolding and illumination of the personal worlds of subjective experience as they emerge at the intersection.

Let us examine a clinical example. A female therapist brought to supervision her discomfort with Yvonne, a young woman whose flirtatious behavior had surfaced that morning in their therapy session. The therapist's dilemma concerned how to make Yvonne conscious of her sexual feelings. The supervisor observed that the therapist was wearing an attractive but very revealing blouse and he wondered whether Yvonne might have been aroused by this. The therapist was surprised by the question, unaware that her sheer blouse might have had some stimulating properties for Yvonne.

Many possibilities are raised by this example. For instance, who was attracted to whom? Was the therapist initiating a same sex flirtation with Yvonne? Did the therapist dress that morning for her opposite sex supervisor later that day? Was the therapist trying to disguise her sexual feelings for her supervisor by focusing on Yvonne's sexuality? And had the supervisor unwittingly set the whole process in motion by his attraction to the supervisee? The point is that an intrapsychic focus leads to an examination of the inner workings of one person's mind, like Yvonne's presumed inner conflicts around same sex attraction, as if they exist in isolation from the whole treatment context. A systemic, contextual focus expands the field of view to incorporate the whole, multileveled therapeutic context, which includes Yvonne, the therapist, and the supervisor.

It might be argued that any good therapist would examine the transference/countertransference implications of this encounter. However, transference and countertransference refer to processes going on within one person's mind. Yvonne's sexualized transference is thought to reside within Yvonne's mind, not as an outgrowth of the intersubjective field. Likewise, the therapist's countertransference might be seen as residing within the therapist's mind and not be a contextual construction involving the intersubjective field comprised of Yvonne/therapist. And where does the participation of the supervisor fall in the transference/countertransference matrix? The supervisor is unlikely to explore the extent to which his attraction to the therapist has trickled down to Yvonne, who now finds herself stimulated and aroused by her therapist (see Buirski and Monroe [2000] for a discussion of the supervisor as chaperone). Since transference and countertransference are essentially viewed as processes going on in interacting isolated minds, Orange's (1995) term "co-transference" better captures the contextual construction or intersecting worlds of personal experience.

We are trying to make two points here. The first is that isolated-mind, Cartesian theorizing (just like contextual thinking) strongly influences how and what we hear. We can only hear what is within our auditory range and what is in our range is shaped by our theoretical understandings and clinical expectations. Our second point is that those who privilege Cartesian, isolated-mind perspectives in their theorizing, may, in practice, function as post-Cartesian contextualists would. When they do adopt a contextualist, experiential world perspective, they do so in contradiction to the theory of mental functioning they espouse.

One area where there seems to be much confusion relates to our understanding of the analytic encounter. Most analysts no longer adhere to traditional notions of the analyst as an anonymous blank screen or the possibility of abstinence and neutrality as analytically realizable stances (Adler and Bachant 1998). There is widespread recognition that the analytic field is impacted by the person of the analyst. Relational theorists refer to the analytic field as being co-constructed, meaning that both parties to the analytic encounter contribute to the experience. To say that all analytic experience is co-constructed, though, does not negate that each member of the analytic dyad brings to the encounter his or her own uniquely formed worlds of experience. Nor does co-construction imply that each participant contributes in equal measure. As Aron (1996) has observed, the analytic relationship is mutual but not symmetrical; it is shaped and regulated by contributions brought by both parties, but not in equal measure.

Like the home run, the analytic encounter is contextually quite complex. The context cannot ever be completely specified, but an important factor in what is ultimately understood is the differing organizations of experience that both analyst and patient bring to their meeting. Some aspects of the analyst's organization of experience that will impact the analytic encounter include her personal world of experience, comprised of her theory and the clinical expectations that derive from theory, her knowledge and experience treating patients, and the state of her personal life, with all its attendant fulfillments and disappointments. For the analysand's part, his organization of experience will include some of the following: his sophistication about psychoanalytic theory and practice, and his expectations of it; that is, what has he read, heard, seen, or been told about psychoanalytic treatment. How can associations be free if part of the context includes what the person anticipates the analyst will think of his productions? And, finally, we cannot minimize the extent to which self and interactive regulation shapes the experience of both participants.

However much we might theoretically acknowledge the constitutive role of context in the shaping of experience, this easily slips away in practice and the comfortable tendency is to resort to isolated-mind constructions, particularly when the heat is on. What is the problem in practice, you might ask, with resorting to isolated-mind constructs anyway? Does it matter whether the earth is the center of the universe or not when your goal is to get to your neighbor's house. This gets to the crux of the matter. Does it really make a difference in clinical practice? We believe that it matters very much and will try to illustrate this with a clinical vignette.

Mary, a single woman in her thirties, is carrying on an affair with a married man. He gives her many expensive gifts and now he offers to buy her a car, which she very much could use. The patient expresses to her therapist feelings of discomfort and shame with being given money. Mary says, "It makes me feel like a prostitute."

What might the therapist make of this association? Perhaps a Kleinian would think, "You envy my money and wish to put your shame at not having money into me." A Freudian might think, "You are drawn to a man like your father who uses money to buy what he wants." A relationalist might think, "Your neediness pulls for him to fill you up." A self psychologist might think, "He must value you a great deal."

We might all agree that, as is the case with most clinical questions, "It depends." But on what does it depend? It depends, we contend, on as much as we can fathom of the context, the intersubjective system, in which this exchange takes place. Both participants are bringing their unique organizations of experience to this moment.

In terms of Mary's world of experience, she is someone who has gotten very little, either of tangible goods or the experience of feeling loved. She deeply longs to be taken care of and to feel valued. Another aspect of Mary's organization of experience concerns her feelings of worthlessness because she never felt treated as lovable and worthy by her parents. This raises the possibility that, along with shame over accepting money, like a prostitute, finally being treated by a man as someone worth giving to might lead Mary to feel proud and valued for her worth to this suitor.

Mary's therapist is a woman of similar age for whom Mary has expressed admiration. She sees her therapist as strong, independent, and confident; traits that Mary feels she lacks. In supervision, the supervisor wondered how the therapist was feeling about Mary. The therapist indicated that she wished to empower Mary so that Mary could feel worthy without debasing herself by accepting payoffs for sex. This suggests that the therapist looks down on Mary for taking expensive gifts, thinking that Mary is, in fact, acting like a prostitute.

By ignoring the intersubjective system and focusing primarily on Mary's isolated mind, the therapist could unwittingly confirm Mary's feeling of shame, neglect her feeling of pride, and overlook Mary's possible transferential need to accommodate to what she experienced as her therapist's expectations of how Mary should feel. That is, Mary's confession to feeling "like a prostitute" might be subtly influenced by her experience of her therapist's disdain.

Mary's association that she feels like a prostitute could have been formed at the interface of their two subjectivities. In this example, both Mary and her therapist may be interactively regulating themselves around uncomfortable feelings of being given to. This interaction between the two participants is not the expression of conflict within the mind of either party alone. Mary's subjective experience has been intersubjectively constructed, as has the therapist's. From the intersubjective systems perspective, the therapeutic process might explore the experience of reciprocal influence between Mary and her therapist leading to a broadening of the horizons of both. As supervisors, we assume that this expression of "feeling like a prostitute" emerges, at least in part, from the subjectivity of the therapist. We would encourage the supervisee/therapist to wonder how her subjectivity has intersected with Mary's. We hope that this example has illustrated the complexity of the intersubjective field in structuring what both members of the therapeutic dyad talk about and the feelings that emerge in each.

Therapy is a complicated business, but it is all the more complicated because the therapist's own world of experience is part of the context and so is the other's expectations of the way that the therapist's experience is organized. The fact that it is so difficult to discern all the contextual factors suggests that a stance of fallibilism (Orange, Atwood, Stolorow 1997), of holding one's formulations tentatively, is a wise course.

Thus, while the analytic pair may never be able to sort out all the possible meanings associated with any analytic exchange, we believe that fundamentally analysis is the process of making sense together of the analytic experience, and not of figuring out the patient. Treatment, from this perspective, is about exploring and expanding worlds of personal experience rather than finding and interpreting dynamic truths about the operation of an isolated mind. For as Donna Orange (2002), echoing Winnicott, has proposed, "there is no such thing as a patient, that there is only a patient in the context of the analyst's care, and conversely that there is no such thing as an analyst, but only an analyst for and with this particular patient" (p. 698).

NOTES

1. Donna Orange (2002, p. 698). A similar point has been made by Atwood and Stolorow (1984, p. 65).
2. Max Buirski (personal communication) directed our attention to this dynamic.

Chapter Two

Innocent Analyst or Implicated Analyst

In the ideal empirical world, one could perform an experiment in which an analysand's flow of associations would be held constant and we could observe the impact of various theoretical perspectives and technical interventions on the analysand's subsequent functioning. In a physics experiment, if we control all other variables but vary the angle with which a cue ball strikes an object ball, we would be able to predict with a high degree of confidence the path the object ball will take. In psychotherapy, if we vary the content or timing of an interpretation, we have much less ability to predict the person's likely response. Unfortunately, the psychotherapy process allows for so many undefined and elusive variables that it is extremely difficult for us to perform a controlled experiment.

If we wish to compare the different theoretical and clinical implications of psychotherapy practiced from an intrapsychic, isolated-mind perspective with an intersubjective systems perspective, we must be resigned to accept that this cannot be done with a controlled experiment. Since one cannot prove or disprove the merits of one approach or the other with reference to a single case, we must make do with argument and analysis. In an effort to highlight the various implications of intrapsychic, isolated-mind, objectivist notions and intersubjective systems, contextual notions on the process of treatment, I will make extensive reference to the report of several sessions from a single clinical case.

The case report I have chosen was presented by Martin Silverman, MD. (1987). Silverman wrote the case description in response to an invitation to present clinical material for a discussion on how theory shapes technique. Silverman's clinical material, which included excerpts from four consecutive treatment sessions, interspersed with observations of his own thought process, was then the subject of discussion by eight analysts representing varying theoretical perspectives, not including the intersubjective systems perspective. Since Silverman accepted the invitation to present this case material with the expectation that others would critique it, I do not feel I am taking unfair advantage by adding the intersubjective systems perspective to the mix. My task here, then, is necessarily hypothetical and speculative: to use Silverman's rich and detailed material to speculate on the differential impacts that intrapsychic, isolated-mind theorizing and contextual, intersubjective systems perspectives would have on the same clinical material.

This is a chapter on how one's theory of mental functioning shapes one's clinical practice. It is not necessary, for this purpose, to presuppose that Silverman's theoretical perspective or mine is representative of a larger number of adherents or a well-defined school of thought. For the purposes of this chapter, it is only relevant that Silverman and I approach clinical work with different assumptions about the psychogenesis of problems in living and different philosophical worldviews that strongly influence how we think and practice. Writing from my view of the contextual, intersubjective systems perspective, my critique of Silverman's work is unavoidably filtered through the lens of my worldview. And, the same can be said for you, the reader. This, then, is not just a commentary on a field constructed of two participants in a treatment relationship, but a field that is shaped by the writer and the reader as well.

It is important to bear in mind that Silverman wrote this case material for publication in 1987, almost twenty years ago. The influence of relational thinking was not new then; British Object Relations Theory, Interpersonal theory, and Self Psychology had all been extensively discussed in the psychoanalytic literature by that point. Happily, the influence of relational and intersubjective systems perspectives on clinical practice has become even more fully understood, accepted, and integrated into mainstream clinical practice since Silverman reported on his work. Therefore, my critique of Silverman's clinical material must also be viewed in the historical context in which it appears. It is possible that, were Silverman to treat Miss K today, his work would incorporate more of a relational mindset.

Silverman located the model of the mind from which he derived his clinical work as the structural model. He described the structural model as follows:

> [I]it emphasizes the concepts of innate libidinal and aggressive drives; heuristic division into id, ego, and superego as systematized, mental and emotional operational groupings; progressive ego development that in part is conflict-free but in very large part is conflict-derived and defensive in nature; emotional devel-

opment through more or less well-defined developmental phases and subphases; and relationships with people that derive from the confluence of internal desire and external impingement (Silverman 1987, pp. 277–78).

As Haglund and I have discussed in chapter 1, this structural model fits comfortably within an isolated-mind view of mental life (Stolorow and Atwood 1992). I will refer to Silverman as "the analyst" in the body of this chapter since my aim is not to critique the person, but to illustrate the way that the theory of the analyst influences the intersubjective field of the treatment relationship.

The analyst presented the case of a twenty-five-year-old woman, Miss K, who "showed sexual and social inhibitions, masochistic tendencies, and chronic, neurotic depression" (Silverman 1987, p. 147). She expressed "a litany of complaints and grudges over injuries and slights she could neither forget nor forgive" (p. 147). She considered herself to be dumb and, in relation to her father, she developed a posture of "pseudostupidity." "She was an unhappy, brooding, angry child who felt lonely and different from her peers" (p. 148). After several years of analysis, the analyst judged that Miss K had shown improvement, as indicated by weight loss, moving out of her parents' home, and renewed social interactions with men; unfortunately, these were temporary gains that began to be reversed. The analyst attributed this relapse to the deterioration of her father's health and the marriage of her beloved older brother. In the analyst's opinion, Miss K "settled into what began to look like an interminable analysis in which she would intellectually explore and understand her conflicts, but would make no real changes in herself or in her way of life" (p. 149).

From just this portion of the case description, I detect a tone of disdain, perhaps even contempt, for Miss K. Rather than merely descriptive, the use of the phrase "litany of complaints" sounds irritable and intolerant. To characterize Miss K as someone who "would intellectually explore and understand her conflicts, but would make no real changes in herself or in her way of life" sounds as if the analyst is impatient and frustrated with Miss K for failing to improve. He seems to be blaming her, as if her aim is to thwart his well-intentioned efforts.

The analyst formulated the main dynamic that was preventing treatment gains this way: "A transference neurosis appeared to develop, in which she expected me, as her analyst, to serve as a quasi-parental, idealized, yet perennially disappointing love object who would care for, protect, and excite her at a controlled, safe distance for the rest of her life, rather than courageously pursuing an uncertain, unpredictable, inevitably imperfect, and therefore partially disappointing real life in the real world" (Silverman 1987, p. 149). In discussing this "transference impasse" in the next paragraph, the analyst commented that he helped Miss K see that, "She had elected to transform her analytic relationship with me into a neurotic substitute both for real life and for resolution of the defensive constellation with which she perpetuated the neurotic compromise-formations that had been impeding her from achieving a truly adult, self-expressing, reasonably satisfying life" (p. 155).

Reflecting on this characterization of Miss K, the analyst uses words and phrases like "she expected me," "rather than courageously," and "she had elected," which imply that Miss K has exercised choice in creating her own misery. It seems odd for someone who identifies with a deterministic theory that places unconscious, intrapsychic conflict at the heart of ones troubles to describe Miss K as someone who chooses to be unhappy. These characterizations have the flavor of blaming and pathologizing Miss K, perhaps because she has had the temerity to get worse instead of better. If she is getting worse with the treatment, it must be her fault for "expecting," "electing," and lacking "courage."

Commonly, isolated-mind notions are called into play around the familiar construct of transference. Traditional notions of transference center on the idea that certain dynamics or conflicts within the individual are a product of unconscious, intrapsychic processes. Invariably, because of some biological or psychological need to repeat, these conflicts are presumed to get played out with other people, especially the analyst. In the form of displacements or projections, these transferences are evidence of the patient's denial, distortion, or falsification of some objectively knowable reality.

From the foregoing material, we can see the strong influence of isolated-mind notions on the analyst's formulation of Miss K's transference. First of all, the analyst seemed to be viewing Miss K from the perspective of an objective external observer. He saw her issues as residing in her isolated mind and gave no recognition to his participation in the treatment context. For example, the analyst apparently believed that Miss K's view of him as a "perennially disappointing love object" (Silverman 1987, p. 149) was a distortion of some truer reality of which the analyst has special knowledge. Miss K's analyst apparently accepted without question that he was an innocent, accurate, objective observer. He seemed not to have entertained the possibility that something of Miss K's experience of him might actually have fit; that he was implicated in the meanings Miss K was making of her experiential world. Second, the analyst seemed to be blaming and pathologizing Miss K for her experience and was judgmental and deprecating of her struggles. He reported having been irritated by her "litany of complaints" and criticized her intellectual defenses and her unwillingness to make real changes in her life. He judged her for not "courageously pursuing an uncertain, unpredictable, inevitably imperfect, and therefore partially disappointing real life in the real world" (p. 149). In fact, her analyst seemed to pathologize Miss K because he believed she deliberately "elected" to foil his treatment aims ("transform her analytic relationship") and "perpetuated the neurotic compromise-formations." The analyst appeared to hold the theoretical notion that it gratified some, perhaps hostile, wish of Miss K's to frustrate the treatment aims of her analyst, at the expense of sacrificing some other, healthier, routes to personal happiness. This formulation, that Miss K would get more pleasure from frustrating her analyst than striving for personal happiness, was consistent with the analyst's description of Miss K as masochistic.

While the analyst could be credited with having shared with the reader his human reactions to Miss K, he did not share with the reader any of his insights into his irritation with and blame of Miss K. Since he did not appear to be working from the perspective that he and Miss K constructed together the experience of the treatment for both, he did not have access to a contextual appreciation of how his experience of Miss K might have contributed to Miss K's experience of him or the treatment. Later though, when discussing the series of sessions, the analyst observed, "There's tightness in my belly, and I'm getting irritated at her excruciating stopping and starting and hesitating" (Silverman 1987, p. 155). This was presented as a reasonable and understandable reaction to Miss K's presentation and not as a feeling state that in any way might have impacted Miss K's experience or the manner of her engagement with him.

From an intersubjective systems perspective, one would want to examine the treatment context for clues to the experience of both members of the analytic dyad. One would not jump to the conclusion that Miss K's apparent turn for the worse was precipitated by the father's deteriorating health and the brother's marriage, factors external to the treatment relationship, without also exploring whether there was any action of the analyst that contributed to Miss K's experience of loss or abandonment. This illustrates how the analyst's theory governs his practice. If it was not within the analyst's isolated-mind theoretical purview to examine his contribution to Miss K's experience and to the intersubjective field, then he could only look to something external to both as the cause. As an alternative to blaming and pathologizing Miss K for her regressive, neurotic compromise-formation, the analyst might have appreciated Miss K's longing to find a new and reparative relationship with him.

Let us now turn to the four sessions presented by the analyst to examine the influence of isolated-mind notions on the course of treatment. The report of Friday's session (the first) began with Miss K saying, "I didn't want to come today. I've been mad at you all week" (Silverman 1987, p. 157). The analyst appeared to have remained silent in response to this comment. As an isolated-mind theorist, perhaps the analyst assumed some transferential distortion was at work within Miss K and he was silently waiting to see further evidence of it. As contextualists, we would wonder why Miss K had been mad at her analyst all week. What had gone on during the prior sessions that made her feel this way? The analyst offered no perspective on Miss K's feeling mad, so we are left to speculate from the material he gave us, as to his contribution to this contextual construction. Perhaps the irritation and frustration that characterized the analyst's description of Miss K prior to reporting the week's process might have played a part. As contextualists, we might have enquired at this point, "You said you didn't want to come today and that you have been mad at me all week—what is my part in your feeling mad at me?" This hypothetical intervention reflects the contextualist view that Miss K's feeling mad could very well have been instigated by something that went on between the two participants, and is likely not just the product of her internal conflicts and defenses being displaced onto the innocent analyst. This would take the discussion beyond the area circumscribed by transference/countertransference, subject/object, internal/external, and into the realm of context or intersubjective system.

Miss K continued, "It's not that I'm mad at you. I wanted to stay away from all this stuff I think I feel here" (Silverman 1987, p. 157). It was curious that Miss K first stated and then needed to retract and disavow her "mad" feeling. She appeared to have some new insight into her mad feelings even though she apparently lacked this awareness during the week. Of course, our suspicions are aroused when Miss K says "I *think* I feel," which suggests her superficial verbal compliance with some imagined expectation of the analyst's. It raised the question of whether this was truly a new insight or just her way of placating her analyst. From an isolated-mind perspective, since the thought "I wanted to stay away from all this stuff" came to Miss K's mind at a particular moment, it would be considered a "free" association that must contain some truth about Miss K. However, from a contextualist perspective, while we don't doubt that it contains some information about Miss K's motives, we nevertheless question whether her insight is a strictly free association or one that derives from the larger context. Might Miss K be paying lip service to some interpretation that had been previously given to her? Perhaps some light will be shed on this by Miss K's next associations.

As the session goes on, the analyst interpreted her need to avoid the feelings she experienced in therapy. This did not appear to be the first time that this interpretation was given. What had seemed like Miss K's own insight may actually have been her repeating an interpretation she had previously been given in order to continue to disavow her mad feeling. If this is the case, then we might speculate that Miss K could not risk being mad at her analyst and needed to accommodate to and please him. In other words, Miss K might have colluded with her analyst in blaming herself by agreeing to attribute her mad feelings to some need to avoid other feelings. This formulation maintains her analyst's innocence as an instigator of her mad feeling. It attributes Miss K's mad feeling to some intrapsychic process going on strictly within her mind that was unrelated to any interpersonal interaction with her analyst. Of course, such self-blame would be the hallmark of masochism. It therefore appears that Miss K has learned that to maintain her connection to her analyst, she has to disavow her angry feelings and placate him by mouthing his interpretations. Rather than the treatment having uncovered Miss K's underlying masochism, it has actually fostered such behavior. Miss K is not "masochistic" in the sense of seeking out pleasure in pain. Instead, her self-defeating or maladaptive behaviors can be understood as the price she is prepared to pay to maintain needed ties to the analyst and probably others.

Miss K continued the theme of feeling anger (which she had just disavowed as being directed toward her analyst) by talking about her anger at her roommate, whom she described as uninterested in her experience. The sequence of associations suggested that in place of her disavowed anger at her analyst, she was now expressing anger felt toward her roommate! Might it be safer for Miss K to express mad feelings toward her roommate, who was not present, than to verbalize anger to her analyst face to face? As if to highlight the contrast, Miss K described her appreciation for her roommate's boyfriend who, unlike her roommate and her analyst, seemed to be affectively attuned to Miss K's experience.

After the talk about her anger at her roommate, Miss K went on to recall other thoughts she had on her way to her session. She reported how she was kept waiting for two hours by her hairdresser and how she expressed her anger when she paid her bill. Her analyst shared his association that, "She'll get a bill from me in a few days, and it's the end of the week and she has to wait two days to see me again on Monday—like the two hrs. for the hairdresser—and in two weeks I leave for vacation, and she'll have to wait a month for me" (Silverman 1987, p. 152). This was a very interesting association on the part of the analyst. Miss K referred to paying a bill and the analyst associated to his bill. Miss K mentioned "two days" and the analyst associated to what "two" meant to him in terms of Miss K's contact with him. This seemed to follow the time-worn psychoanalytic principle that whatever the patient says, it has, on some unconscious level, to do with the analyst. Perhaps it did; however, this is not a formula or a rule but a guideline to be evaluated case by case. Nevertheless, the point of Miss K's association was that she had been kept waiting, which seemed to mean having been treated by the hairdresser as if her time and her needs were of secondary importance. Her analyst can only think of the possible irrational transference meanings that this had for Miss K—how unreasonable it would be of her to resent his fee or his vacation—not how she might have felt he treated her as if her time and life were of secondary importance to his fee and his vacation.

From the intersubjective systems perspective, affects, like thoughts, are also co-constructed. The interaction with the analyst may very well have contributed to Miss K feeling mad. However, Miss K has made no conscious reference to the analyst. If we remove the omniscience of the analyst, then we have no way of knowing whether the analyst's associations are not just about aspects of himself that Miss K may have stirred up. The assumptions of unconscious meanings are as applicable to the analyst as to Miss K. This highlights another difference between the intersubjective systems approach and the modern Freudian perspective. The intersubjective systems perspective focuses on the person's *lived experience*. As Lichtenberg, Lachmann, and Fosshage (1992) point out, "*The message contains the message.* Listening involves appreciating the nuances of the *delivered* message for what is stated, what is implied, what is consciously intended, and what might be unconsciously meant as well" (p. 215). By presuming, as her analyst did, that Miss K's feelings were being displaced from him onto the haircutter, what got neglected was Miss K's subjective experience of having been treated badly by the haircutter and also by him.

Looked at through the lens of intersubjective systems, this train of Miss K's associations about her haircutter was consistent with the roommate theme that "She only thinks of herself" (Silverman 1987, p. 152). We might speculate that Miss K has organized her experience around the notion that she is unimportant and that others have no interest in her. Now, her analyst may become assimilated into this organization of experience but it does not happen in a vacuum or an isolated mind. The analyst's blaming, pathologizing, and irritation with Miss K might have conveyed to her that he was out of touch with her experience. Her anger, then, would not have been a transference distortion of the displacement or projection type; rather, it would have been an affective reaction to her subjectively felt, lived experience of narcissistic injury.

The analyst appeared to connect Miss K's anger with himself, attributing it to Miss K's anger at having to wait two days to see him again and her anger at his summer vacation. In other words, Miss K's anger was understood as a transferential overreaction to the analyst's coming vacation and was therefore an unreasonable distortion of reality. The analyst was thereby exculpated and remained the innocent analyst. Miss K may have had some feeling about their approaching separation, but nothing in any material that the analyst had presented so far bore on this. These were associations of the analyst's and seemed to be driven by his theoretical expectations of how a person would feel about an impending separation. They do not appear to have derived from anything Miss K was quoted as saying. It was equally plausible that instead of anger over separation from the analyst, Miss K might have been feeling relief. This was an example of how theory-based expectations of content and meaning often have a powerful influence on the analyst's interventions and interpretations and may be quite distant from the analysand's lived experience. Because the analyst's theory led him to expect certain transference configurations, his interpretations had the quality of bending Miss K's experience to fit with his expectations.

Miss K continued with associations to how intimidated she felt by her hairdresser and her tennis pro, whom she had begun taking lessons from. If our earlier suspicions that Miss K's anger at the analyst and her retraction and disavowal of these affects were related to her experience of having been blamed and pathologized by the analyst, then her next associations to being intimidated by two men in her life might offer some confirmation.

Miss K continued: "I get intimidated with men. I always feel that they know, they have the knowledge. They have the brains and I'm dumb. . . . It's the same thing here. . . . I feel you're always a step ahead of me. You *know*, because you're smarter than I am" (Silverman 1987, p. 152). The analyst then said, "I don't think that's what it is. I think you feel I know because I'm a man, that as a woman you don't have the brains" (p. 153). Here, the analyst has unwittingly confirmed Miss K's feared experience by negating her formulation and replacing it with his own, thereby showing that he did know better than she. Even if Miss K had the feeling that men knew better, her analyst had just demonstrated that he, a man, knew better, thereby confirming the subjective validity of her beliefs. How do we generalize to the category of all men, when this man in particular was enacting with her the very dynamic that he was attributing to the workings of her isolated mind?

In response to this interpretation, Miss K said, "Do you think I signal it to them and that drives them away? So they think, 'Who wants her!'" (Silverman 1987, p. 153). In reaction to her analyst's knowing better than she, Miss K reverted to blaming and pathologizing herself, as we have seen her do before. Miss K continued, "I think it started in a way when my father said to me, 'Every man is going to want the same thing from you.' I got so angry" (p. 153). Here Miss K seemed to be referring to her father's inference that men will only want her for sex. This had led her to reject men whom she suspected wanted only sex from her and to question the appropriateness of her own sexual desires. The analyst was silent in response to this series of associations. From the intersubjective systems perspective, one would be inclined to affirm Miss K's right to sexual feelings and to reassure her that being desired sexually does not preclude that a man could also value her for other attributes. After all, any man who will love her as a person will also, one hopes, desire sexual intimacy with her. Here was a lost opportunity to mirror and affirm Miss K's sexuality and her desirability, to depathologize her view of herself, and to offer an alternative to her father's attempt to discredit her sexuality and the men who are sexually interested in her.

Miss K then went on to talk about her feeling of being intimidated by both men and women. It was all very confusing to her, and she concluded by saying, "I can't figure it out. There's no rhyme or reason. I don't understand it" (Silverman 1987, p. 153). The analyst then made the following interpretation, "So long as you take that attitude, so long as you don't think it out and find out the rhyme and reason" (Silverman 1987, p. 153). This sounds quite critical and disapproving. Miss K was being blamed and criticized for failing to figure herself out. However, from a contextualist perspective, we would question whether Miss K's confusion might have been derived from her analyst's failure to provide a mirroring and affirming presence. It makes sense that Miss K became disorganized and confused in response to her analyst's silent failure to mirror and affirm her. In reaction to her confusion and disorganization, her analyst became blaming and critical.

In an effort to defend herself, while still confused by the analyst's blaming and criticizing, Miss K protested, "Well, *he* cut my hair. He *cut* me. But she just put her fingers into my hair. I don't understand" (Silverman 1987, pp. 153–54). The analyst interpreted, "He stuck scissors into your hair and she stuck her fingers into your hair. You were talking before that about avoiding sexual excitement. Scissors and fingers into your hair *sounds* sexual" (p. 154), meaning this sounded sexual to the analyst. This was a theory-driven interpretation. One of the problems with Freudian-based theories is the notion that if something Miss K said sounds like a sexual reference to the analyst, then it must mean that sex lies behind Miss K's remark. This instance, however, was all about the analyst's associations, not Miss K's. The analyst had associated to the sexual meanings of the haircut to him and confidently attributed it to Miss K. Miss K clearly felt misunderstood by this interpretation and protested, "Yes. But there's something that doesn't fit" (p. 154).

After her protest, Miss K immediately associated to a masturbation fantasy that she had told to the analyst earlier in the treatment. As contextualists, we have to marvel at the lengths Miss K will go to please her analyst by disavowing her own rejection of his interpretations. Perhaps out of a wish to please or placate him, Miss K produced associations that would satisfy his need to find sexual material. One has to question whether the sexual interpretations the analyst had made did not exert a strong influence on Miss K to follow his lead and associate to a masturbation fantasy. But before he discussed the fantasy, the analyst noted that "I found her slow, start-and-stop delivery agonizing" (Silverman 1987, p. 154). Might this sharing with the reader of his experience of displeasure with Miss K, that her delivery was agonizing, actually be the analyst's reaction to having had his interpretation rejected? Was he frustrated and angry with her for failing to comply or accommodate?

But let us examine this masturbation fantasy for what it might tell us about the intersubjective field. "There's—a doctor—a mad scientist—and his nurse and—he ties me down to—do things to me" (Silverman 1987, p. 154). The analyst interpreted about the hairdresser and the hair washer: "They're the mad scientist doctor and his nurse" (p. 154). It is almost a rule of Freudian-based treatments that should the analysand, Miss K, associate to a doctor, the analyst would suspect that this association contained a transferential reference to him. Surprisingly, such a thought appears never to have crossed the analyst's mind, as he apparently could not imagine that he might have been experienced as the mad scientist who was wildly interpreting sexual contents.

Miss K ignored the analyst's interpretation and continued: "The fantasy had to do with—something—it had to do with getting bigger breasts. It's foolish—I feel sheepish. . . . It's so silly" (Silverman 1987, p. 154). The analyst quickly negated Miss K's experience: "There's nothing silly about it" (p. 154). Miss K acquiesced, "You're right" (p. 154). The analyst then asked, "And what happens to sheep?" (p. 154). Miss K replied, "They get sheared, their hair cut off" (p. 154). The analyst then interpreted, "And so do fallen women" (p. 154).

Miss K has been beaten down. The analyst noted that "The emotion's gone from her voice" (Silverman 1987, p. 155). The analyst interpreted that "You're getting away to avoid uncomfortable feelings" (p. 155), to which Miss K submitted, "You're right" (p. 155). The analyst continued to interpret her avoidance of his insights into the sexual meaning of her associations: "Notice you're interrupting yourself, stopping yourself?" (p. 155). To this Miss K replied, "I don't want to talk about it, think about it; I'm afraid you'll think I'm foolish. I had to submit to the mad scientist, like I was his slave and he was my master" (p. 155). The case can be made that the analyst was the intimidating man whom she struggled to assert herself with and stand up to; the mad scientist to whom she was forced to submit.

The analyst interpreted, with increased vigor, what he perceived as Miss K's defenses against feeling. Finally he said, "You want *me* to be the mad scientist doctor forcing and hurting you and making changes in you" (Silverman 1987, p. 155). To which Miss K, to her credit, replied, "I have to reject that. I can't agree with you on that. That would mean I don't really want to change. But I do want to change (then she again wavers in the face of disagreeing with her analyst, saying) I'll have to think about it" (pp. 155–56).

The analyst shared his final thoughts with the reader: "The thing with the tennis teacher was on the weekend; here's another weekend; in a few weeks

I'll leave her not just for a weekend but for a month; absence makes the heart grow fonder; she also wants to kill me for leaving her, for not being crazy about her so I can't bear to be without her; masochistic transference; transference neurosis" (Silverman 1987, p. 156). Again, we are presented with the analyst's theory-driven associations to the patient's material. Adhering, as he has indicated, to the structural theory of the mind, which views human motivation as deriving from sexual and aggressive id wishes and the ego defenses against them, the analyst imagined first that Miss K, despite her denials, had sexual desires for him. However, it was the analyst's own association, that "absence makes the heart grow fonder." From his associations, it is just as plausible that the analyst might find the analysand sexually attractive, as it is to presume, from her associations, that Miss K is giving disguised voice to her attraction for the analyst.

Working from a dual-drive theory of sex and aggression, the analyst now introduced another theory-driven construction, that Miss K held aggressive impulses toward him. This was evident in his theory-generated conviction that Miss K wished to "kill" him, despite her never having indicated such desires. Part of the difficulty for Miss K is that her spoken denial or unspoken silence is equated with her unconscious confirmation. Yes is yes and no is yes. It is not clear that there was anything Miss K could have said to the analyst to shake his conviction about the transferential nature of her sexual and aggressive impulses.

In his parting association, the analyst demonstrated his commitment to an isolated-mind view of treatment when he pronounced that Miss K had a masochistic transference, as if she had wished to be hurt by him. Rather than wishing to be hurt, the argument could be made that Miss K had indeed been hurt by her analyst's misattunement and theory-driven interpretations that reflected how out of touch he was with her experience.

The analyst's final thoughts for the session are worth examining further. The intersubjective systems perspective strongly endorses the notion that analyst and analysand contribute to the co-construction of experience for both parties to the encounter. For an analyst working from the intersubjective systems perspective, the analyst needs always to be alert to his potential impact and influence on structuring the other's experience. In the session-ending fragment above, the analyst appeared to be addressing Miss K's experience of him. However, the analyst, while imagining the sexual and aggressive feelings Miss K had for him, was not examining his contribution to a co-construction of Miss K's experience of him. Rather, he was fantasizing about the meaning he had come to have for Miss K as if he was an objective, detached observer, seeing the presumed meanings as originating solely from deep within her isolated, unconscious mind. He remained the objective evaluator of her experience, safely assured that he was innocent of playing any part in the construction of that experience. From an intersubjective systems perspective, one wonders whether his objective observer and interpreter stance has not contributed to Miss K's experience of him, implicating the analyst as the "mad scientist" who does things to her, without understanding her.

The second session (Monday) began with Miss K reporting that she had received a phone call from a thirty-nine-year-old man whose personal ad she responded to. She felt pleased and flattered. The man apparently thought her reply was funny. "It was wonderful" (Silverman 1987, p. 156), she said. Next, Miss K talked about a tennis lesson that she enjoyed. "I have good hand-eye coordination. . . . It was good for my ego" (p. 156). These affirming, self-esteem boosting experiences enabled her to muster the courage to go to a singles dance. At the dance, she met a man who asked her on a date. She reported a few more positive, affirming experiences. Then Miss K said, "I was sitting in the waiting room and thinking that I didn't do much more on the weekend. Wanted to be alone. . . . Friday [the first session in the reported sequence], here, I opened up and went into something, and now I hear myself rambling about the dance and nothing consequential" (p. 157). The analyst observed, "You sound undecided about looking further, thinking and feeling further, into what you opened up on Friday" (p. 157).

This is an interesting sequence. Miss K began the session feeling proud and perhaps a bit expansive, energized, about several affirming experiences she has had. Then, after remembering Friday's session, in which the analyst had suggested that she masochistically wished not to change, she started to get self-critical and ended by accusing herself of rambling and producing inconsequential associations. Apparently, feeling proud and expansive was "nothing consequential." Did Miss K believe that the analyst could not share her sense of pleasure in her accomplishments and was only interested in her failings? Were these self-critical comments truly free associations or were they perhaps in response to her memory of the analyst having found fault with her. She seemed to be beating him to the blaming punch by beating up on herself. The analyst picked up this line of self-criticism. However, he missed an opportunity to affirm her prior good feeling and her pride and explore with her how quickly it dissolved in the face of her anticipation of his criticism. This is a good example of an intersubjective system in which Miss K's central affect state may have been destabilized by her anticipation of her analyst's criticism.

In response to the analyst's implied criticism of her for avoiding Friday's material, Miss K associated to the film *Now, Voyager*, a movie the analyst described as "about a *doctor* (his emphasis, indicating that now he believes he is this 'good' doctor, not the unflattering 'mad scientist' doctor) rescuing her from her mother" (Silverman 1987, p. 157). Miss K associated to how she has been criticized and blamed, by her father and the first tennis pro, but how the second tennis instructor was complimentary and supportive and she could learn from him. She described the psychiatrist in the movie as similarly attuned, available, and supportive. These were selfobject experiences that enhanced her self-esteem and promoted self-cohesion. She wished the analyst would be more like Claude Raines, the psychiatrist in the movie. Her analyst interpreted that she wished to turn him into her father and, through a transference distortion, saw him as critical and disapproving (a return to the masochism theme he has been pursuing). Miss K protested, "I don't want to make you into my father" (p. 158). The analyst, disconfirming her plea, returned to his preferred theme that Miss K wanted to turn him into the "mad scientist" who would give her bigger breasts. Miss K talked about not having big breasts and therefore not being attractive to men. "I'm so mad and jealous. I can't help thinking what could men see in me" (p. 159). The analyst seemed quite interested in this talk of big breasts. It fit with the Oedipal theme he had been developing about Miss K's relationship with her father. He reported thinking to himself,

> So *Now, Voyager* has something to do with a daddy doctor taking her away, carrying her off with him, leaving mother behind. So I am supposed to cure her by being her idealized, loving father, leaving my wife/her mother, and marrying her; the mad-scientist doctor giving her bigger breasts is really giving her mother's breasts? Finding her more attractive than her mother? She repeatedly brings up *Now, Voyager.* Is that the script for the analysis? (p. 159).

In this session, the analyst has single-mindedly attended to his theory-driven understanding that Miss K's associations to *Now, Voyager* are about her Oedipal longings and her wish for the analyst to be the desired father. Nowhere does the analyst cite any material that suggests Miss K wishes to steal him or her father from their wives. Rather, all of Miss K's associations to the film seemed to be consistent with her wish to be treated as affirmatively as Claude Raines treated Bette Davis, "He's soft spoken, all-knowing in a quiet way, not dominating, but giving her the time, not hurrying her" (Silverman 1987, p. 158). Miss K seemed to be longing for affirming and self-delineating selfobject functions (Stolorow 1994) that neither her father, nor her analyst, had been able or, in her experience, willing to provide. So the analyst was sadly correct when he snidely observed, "So I'm supposed to cure her by being her idealized, loving father" (Silverman 1987, p. 159). Yes. Miss K has been struggling to communicate her longing for missed developmental experiences of affirmation and validation. Instead of finding the selfobject relationship she has long been seeking, Miss K has encountered a misattuned parental substitute who has criticized, blamed, and pathologized her for being masochistically stuck.

There is a good deal of confusion and contradiction to Miss K's associations in this and other sessions. She has a tendency to say something and then disavow it. She expresses an affect and then repudiates it. This might be due, as her analyst's theory would suggest, to intrapsychic conflict between wish and defense. However, the material of the sessions lends itself to another interpretation. That is, that Miss K has been indoctrinated by her analyst's theory-driven understanding and interpretation of her experience. He has apparently made interpretations to her that she felt she must submit and accommodate to: for example, "When I get so mad, it's a substitute, I'm beginning to see, for being sexually excited" (Silverman 1987, p. 158); "You're right; I feel time is running out. I want to goad my father and make him mad" (p. 158); and "We've talked about my being overweight as taking out on my body my anger at my body" (p. 159). I would propose that the analyst's theory-driven pathologizing and blaming interpretations and characterizations have repeated the destructive interactions she had become accustomed to with her father. Miss K's treatment with her analyst has undermined Miss K's sense of self-delineation and self-coherence, much the way her self-organization was thwarted and damaged by her father. Far from transferentially displacing her anger at her father onto her innocent analyst, Miss K's analyst has treated her all too similarly to her father, and she has good justification for feeling angry.

The third session (Tuesday) found Miss K beginning with, "I know I have to go back to where I was yesterday" (Silverman 1987, p. 159). Apparently Miss K has learned that not following her analyst's agenda incurs his disapproval. This sounds like Miss K felt that to win her analyst's approval she had to accommodate to his expectations or face criticism for being resistant and difficult. The good analysand (girl) picks up where she left off the previous session; the difficult analysand (girl) follows her own agenda.

Miss K did return to the prior theme of being unattractive to men. Growing up, she "wanted to be taller, have bigger breasts, be a model" (Silverman 1987, p. 159). She reported that her mother disparaged the glamorous women she wished to be like (models, stewardesses) as glorified waitresses who were not good enough. By implication, Miss K was a failure for wanting to be like them. Miss K also had fantasies of becoming a nurse but her mother discouraged her, implying that she was not smart enough to handle the sciences. Miss K felt that her mother fed her false hope that she would grow into an attractive woman, which simultaneously undermined her precarious self-worth. She gave several examples of how her self-esteem was damaged and how she tried to compensate for feeling worthless with vicarious, antidotal fantasies of getting attention and being desired.

Throughout this part of the session, the analyst reported being largely silent, despite sharing some critical and disapproving thoughts about Miss K with the reader. In response to Miss K expressing her wish to "fit in with, and be popular" (Silverman 1987, p. 160), the analyst made the first reported intervention of this section of the session, saying, "And you wanted to be different" (p. 160) (from how she felt she was). This reflected the analyst's first reported nonjudgmental attempt to attune to Miss K's subjective experience. Understandably, Miss K heard this intervention as attuned and immediately confirmed this by saying, "I wanted to be queen of the hill" (p. 160). This brief attuned intervention, especially in the absence of any critical or blaming comments, allowed Miss K to continue to discuss her low self-worth. Tellingly, Miss K said, "There are lingering memories of times I started to feel good about myself and then got slammed in the face for it, and it made it that much harder to try the next time" (p. 160). Interestingly, the analyst, who repeatedly questioned whether Miss K was talking about him when there might be some sexual or Oedipal implication, did not register that this observation might have been a comment on their relationship—that Miss K felt slammed by him.

Miss K reported, "I'm moved by handicapped people who overcome their handicaps. I see myself as a handicapped person" (Silverman 1987, p. 161). At this point, the analyst contradicted her and offered his alternative version of what she was feeling; "Or maybe it's more like Claude Raines and Bette Davis" (p. 162). The analyst has changed the subject by reintroducing a topic of interest to him: the film relationship between the psychiatrist and patient and the transference love implied. Miss K caught his drift. She replied, trying to disconfirm the implied sexual striving, "She had strong, fond feelings for the psychiatrist. He helped her turn her life around and get free. I relate to her. . . . I fantasize that happening: I'm going to be transformed" (p. 162). "By me?" queried her analyst, clearly incredulous that he might be expected to engage in a curative emotional relationship. "Who else?" replied Miss K. Responding to further observations Miss K had made about the film, her analyst observed, "You weren't satisfied with whom she ended up with" (p. 162). Miss K said, "I know what you're getting at, that I wanted her to end up with her psychiatrist, and the same with me" (p. 162). Here Miss K was again aware that her analyst was pressing his transference interpretation on her; that she wished to be with him, sexually no doubt. This was a totally misattuned interpretation of her longings that Miss K indeed had the courage to reject. She replied, "It wasn't her psychiatrist who gave her courage to go on, but Paul Heinred, who sent her flowers when she was trying to get the courage to leave her mother" (p. 162). In other words, Miss K was saying that it was the other male character who also provided needed selfobject functions, functions that she wished her analyst would provide. The wish for a selfobject relationship was misconstrued by the analyst into being a wish for a sexual relationship. This again was a misunderstanding driven by the expectations of structural theory, rather than the clinical material.

Miss K continued with the theme of her wish for a selfobject relationship with her psychiatrist. Miss K confessed, "I'm never completely relaxed here" (Silverman 1987, p. 162). Her analyst interpreted, based on his theoretical expectations, "Because your feelings make you nervous" (p.162). With this theory-driven interpretation, the analyst was again pressing the point that it was her transferential sexual feelings for him that made her uncomfortable. Miss K, under pressure to accommodate, acquiesced by saying, "I guess so" (p. 162). She now associated to "my fear of my feelings" (p. 162) with another young man. However, it was far from clear that the feelings she described being afraid of were sexual. In fact, this association had the tone of a pathological accommodation (Brandchaft 1994) to the demands she experienced her analyst placing on her. The analyst pressed on, "And you're afraid of your feelings and how strong they are here with me" (Silverman 1987, p. 162). To this interpretation, Miss K made the hallmark statement of the defeated person who has been badgered into compliance with an incorrect interpretation: "I think so; must be so" (p. 162). The analyst, perhaps recognizing Miss K's pathological compliance, launched into a long, rambling interpretation, trying to pull together all his prior interpretations about Miss K's associations to the film *Now, Voyager* as being about her defenses against her sexual, Oedipal longings for him and her wishes that he love her.

It is very likely that Miss K would experience her analyst's relentless pursuit of the Oedipal theme as a massive misattunement to her longing for a selfobject relationship. The analyst himself reported feeling uncomfortable with his last interpretive attempt. Finally, he resolved his doubts about the hurtful impact of his interpretation, his sadism, by blaming it on Miss K: "Am I afraid of my sadism she's masochistically inviting?" The analyst acted like the ocean tide—the innocent analyst whose sadism is wrenched from him by the masochistic pull of Miss K's gravitational field.

Is there any way to ascertain whether the analyst is correct in his supposition that Miss K is defending against her Oedipal transference; or, the alternative view taken here, that Miss K feels forced to accommodate to the "mad scientist," despite wishing for a developmentally needed selfobject relationship? One way to answer this question would be to take the traditional psychoanalytic approach to evidence by looking at what happens next in the process.

No session was scheduled on Wednesday, and on Thursday, Miss K canceled her appointment because she was ill. Canceling because of illness could be viewed, from an isolated-mind perspective, as a manifestation of Miss K's resistance in reaction to a supposed accurate interpretation that her analyst had made in Tuesday's session; that is, a negative therapeutic reaction, where in the face of an accurate, health-promoting interpretation, the person gets worse. From a contextualist perspective, it might have reflected that Miss K was angry at her analyst's massive misattunement in the previous session and had expressed this, in the only safe way she had available, by avoiding the next scheduled appointment. These reflect two very different ways of understanding some aspect of Miss K's behavior. In the first case, it could be a neurotic resistance; in the second case, it could be a healthy, adaptive move toward self-protection.

Miss K arrived for Friday's session, and the analyst reported that she was "angry, sulky, tightlipped, and almost inaudible" (Silverman 1987, p. 163). He went on to speculate, "She's defending against an imagined accusation that she wasn't really ill, looking for a fight" (p. 163). Not one to let go of a theme, the analyst interpreted, "You use anger to push away other feelings" (p. 164). Presumably, the analyst was referring to her Oedipal feelings, which he believes she masks with anger. However, it was striking that it never occurred to him that her anger might have been in reaction to something he had done to her, like hurting her through persistent misattunement and pressure to accommodate to his theory driven interpretations. This reflected a classic, one-person, isolated-mind perspective on the therapeutic relationship. Miss K might certainly have had feelings about her analyst, but they were presumed to come from displaced or projected inner desires. Since the innocent analyst never deserves the anger directed at him, the analysand's anger must be a defense against something else. In this case, the analyst seemed to believe that Miss K was defending, through the defensive maneuver of reaction formation (turning her feelings of love into anger), against her sexual desires for him, which she has displaced onto him from their true object, her father.

The analyst noted that his report of Friday's session was condensed. He ended his report with a long, quite touching, quote from Miss K:

> My father didn't give me what I wanted from him [her analyst hears sex, but I think she means selfobject relating] and I got mad and reacted by taking it out on all men and turning on and turning away from all men; and then I met you and I got mad at you for not giving me what I wanted from him and want from you, and I'm taking out on you what I feel about my father and all men! You're going away and leaving me, and I'm angry and sulking and insisting on being miserable! Am I going to spend my whole life angry and sulking? (Silverman 1987, pp. 164–65).

This is a tour de force of integrating both her own and the analyst's understandings—a marvelous compromise formation. From the analyst's structural theory perspective, Miss K could be confirming her anger at her father and the analyst for withholding their love and frustrating her desire to be the woman in their lives. From the intersubjective systems perspective, Miss K is angry that her father, her brother, and her analyst have all hurt her by being misattuned to her developmental longings for attuned responsiveness. As the analyst outlined in the beginning of the report, "She had always felt unappreciated and mistreated, both at home and outside of it. The details which she presented amounted to a litany of complaints and grudges over injuries and slights she could neither forget nor forgive" (Silverman 1987, p. 147).

Unfortunately, as the analyst has reported, Miss K has been getting worse as treatment has progressed. The analyst described the "transference impasse" (Silverman 1987, p. 149) that was the focus of the year preceding the sample sessions:

> By means of painstaking analytic work, Miss K was helped to see that she had elected to transform her analytic relationship with me into a neurotic substitute both for real life and for resolution of the defensive constellation with which she perpetuated the neurotic compromise-formation that had been impeding her from achieving a truly adult, self-expressing, reasonably satisfying life (p. 149).

By stressing how Miss K "elected" and "perpetuated" her own problems, the blaming, pathologizing stance of the isolated-mind perspective becomes apparent. In this vein, the analyst criticized Miss K for not "courageously pursuing an uncertain, unpredictable, inevitably imperfect, and therefore partially disappointing real life in the real world" (Silverman 1987, p. 149).

In contrast to the analyst's view that Miss K was resistantly foiling his therapeutic efforts, is the view of the sample sessions that the analyst was implicated in repeating with Miss K the same misattuned, hurtful relationship she has had with the other significant figures in her life. Her analyst did not understand her longing for selfobject relatedness, imposed his ideological perspective on her, badgered her with theory-driven interpretations, and promoted her pathological accommodation to his view. Miss K's final plaintive cry, "Am I going to spend my whole life angry and sulking?" (Silverman 1987, p. 165), seems sadly prescient.

In summarizing an intersubjective systems perspective on the clinical material presented by Silverman, what stands out is the limiting effects of the authoritarian, objectivist stance of the isolated-mind position. To the extent that one's commitment to a view of human motivation derives from adherence to a theory of mind, it limits what you hear and the meanings you make of it. The analyst is committed to such a theoretical position and his understanding of Miss K is made to fit with what he believes.

Intersubjective systems, on the other hand, as was discussed in chapter 1, is not a theory of mental functioning that postulates certain universal constructs, like the Oedipus complex or stages of psychosexual development. It is, instead, a sensibility that encourages an examination of the reciprocal mutual influences that the parties to the intersubjective field have on each other. It places the influence of context at the center of any examination of process.

I have tried to delineate the extent and effect of the analyst's theoretical expectations on the unfolding process. If we strip away theory-based observations and interpretations, we get a picture of two people who don't understand each other, frustrate and hurt each other, and struggle to survive the mutual invalidations they experience. Miss K is striving for health, straining to hold onto some sense of self-delineation, integrity, and value in the face of persistent invalidation and usurpation. The analyst is struggling for confirmation of his good intentions and his therapeutic effectiveness. The two seem at an impasse that benefits neither and from which neither can be extricated.

Chapter Three

Two Approaches to Psychotherapy

In chapter 2, I offered an intersubjective systems critique of a clinical case presented by a therapist working from the perspective of contemporary structural theory. There, I speculated on the impact the therapist was having on the process and sought to understand the unfolding of the therapeutic process in terms of the mutual and interactive regulations that grew out of that unique intersubjective field. However, in fairness to Dr. Silverman, there is no way to know, with certainty, how Miss K would have responded to a therapeutic field that contained an intersubjectively oriented psychotherapist.

If only the therapy process lent itself to being studied by the experimental method, we might finally be able to resolve one of the questions that have nagged at therapists for the last one hundred years: whose way of working is most effective for which people? Unfortunately, the psychotherapy process does not lend itself to the systematic control of the variables that affect the process. This is, in large part, because the psychotherapy process involves an open system where many, if not most, of the variables affecting the process cannot be identified. Since the variables that impact the process come from the conscious and unconscious worlds of experience of both participants, the participants themselves may have no awareness of all the factors influencing their engagement.

Since we cannot control variables we can't even identify, one possibility would be to have both participants function as their own controls. Suppose we could have the same therapist participate in two sessions with the same person, where the therapist would work from a different theoretical perspective in each session. Since the subjective world of experience for both participants might be considered constants and only the treatment perspectives would differ, we might then be in a position to observe the differential effects of the therapist's theory on the process.

Obviously, such an undertaking would be fraught with methodological difficulties. However, just such an opportunity occurred serendipitously in an initial interview. In this chapter, I will describe that interview in which I, as the therapist, began working first from the perspective of contemporary structural theory, similar to Silverman's in chapter 2, and then deliberately switched midway through the session to an approach informed by an intersubjective systems sensibility. I will present the verbatim process from this session because I think it illustrates the differential impact on both participants and on the unfolding process of each distinct approach.

When the session began, it was not my aim to switch stances. However, as it progressed, the person I was working with, Mr. G, appeared to become increasingly sullen and withholding. His responses became briefer and more irritable. I found myself feeling frustrated and also irritable. At one point, I heard myself make an uncharacteristically sarcastic remark to Mr. G. Recognizing my hostility, I refocused on the empathic/introspective stance. Expecting that Mr. G would respond with anger to my sarcasm, I was jolted into a fresh awareness and understanding of Mr. G when he reacted unexpectedly. Rather than becoming angry or silent in response to what I felt was my countertransferential hostility, Mr. G responded as if I had made an attuned intervention. The disjunction between Mr. G's experience of me as attuned and my subjective experience of myself as hostile propelled me into a new recognition of the intersubjective field we had created together. This led me to deliberately adopt a different stance, one derived from the intersubjective systems perspective, for the duration of the session. Not surprisingly, as any perturbation to a system will impact the whole system (Thelen and Smith 1994), the shift in my stance seemed to impact Mr. G in a new way and the therapeutic process began to unfold differently.

As the session unfolds, I will share my subjective experience of the process and my subsequent thoughts about what was transpiring. I make no claims to objectivity, either about my own experience or Mr. G's. Nevertheless, in this in vivo experiment, the same people are involved in an interpersonal engagement in which the one made a deliberate decision to relate differently during the two halves of the same session, with interesting outcomes.

MR. G: Oh, boy! (*settling into chair*)

PB: So, why don't you tell me why you've come?

MR. G: Uh, yeah, yeah, okay (*rocking in chair*) . . . that's a hard one but I'm gonna try because, uh, you know I was really scared about coming here. I, uh, I . . . I just got so, so upset about it that I, uh, I, just couldn't sleep last night about the whole thing, but I knew I had to come because things have really gotten bad for me lately—very, very bad. I, uh . . . I, uh . . . I, you know, recently separated from my, from my wife. Actually she left me. And, uh, and I, and I just started feeling so bad about it. In the beginning I was glad but in the last, uh, month or so things have gotten very, very difficult for me. In fact I, uh, I have all kinds of funny things happen to me. My, my . . . I've gotten these palpitations of the heart and so on and so forth, and I, uh, I don't sleep well. I even have nightmares which I never had before. In fact I never had dreams. I just started having these dreams, and they're awful dreams. So I'm very disturbed about that. And, uh, so I was talking to her and trying to get her, you know. . . . I wanted her to see me again because she doesn't want to see me at this point. And she told me that she's in therapy that she said she would try to, uh, get a name, uh, uh, for me to see somebody to get some help. And, I got your name. And, uh, that's how I'm here. I gave you a call and that's how I'm here.

Mr. G seemed to be in a lot of distress. He has responded to his wife's rejection with a variety of somatic symptoms. I wonder whether he has come for therapy because he wants greater understanding of his experience, or because he thinks that this is a way to win his wife's favor.

PB: Well, what do you feel you'd like me to help you with?

I ask this question to test the waters for his willingness to engage in self-exploration.

MR. G: (*laughs*) Boy, that's a good one 'cause, you know, just today, you know, it's amazing something popped into my mind today. I said why, why am I going there? What is it I want? You know, you know what came to me. I said, uh. . . . I want him to get . . . make it so that people will like me. You know what I mean? That's what hit me. I want it so that people will like me . . . start liking me.

Mr. G seems sincerely perplexed by my question ("That's a good one"). My initial reaction was that he was quite defended. Since Mr. G made the appointment several days previously, his comment that one reason for coming popped into his head just to-day suggests that he has not been giving much thought to himself. He seems to be of the impression that therapists fix people. I wonder if Mr. G thinks that he has done his part of the job by appearing in my office and now I am supposed to do my job of some-how fixing him. However, there is something touching about his feeling that people don't like him and his desire for me to make him more likable.

PB: Do you have the experience that people generally haven't liked you?

MR. G: Yeah, that's right. I, uh, I just know that somehow came to me lately, that thing, that fact.

I feel more strongly that Mr. G is saying, "I'm here, now you do something."

PB: Are you feeling that your wife is the most recent example?

My thought is to move from the general, "People don't like me," to the specific case that has brought him to therapy.

MR. G: Uh, well, yeah. I mean, uh, but it seems to me that's the way it's been an awfully long time, now that I start to think about it.

I'm thinking that this line, while certainly quite relevant and important, seems quite distant from his immediate relationship with his wife and whatever feelings he has about what has transpired.

PB: Tell me, first, what led up to the separation?

I have changed the subject and this seems to have unsettled Mr. G. I've asked him to try to make sense of his narrative, which seems like an unfamiliar endeavor for him.

MR. G: Uh, what led up to the separation? Well, uh . . . that's . . . complicated. Um. She . . . she didn't want to have sex anymore, for a long time, you know. And I didn't really, didn't bother me because I'd never really been that interested in sex. In a funny kind of way it had never been that great of a thing for me. And she wanted it more than I did. And uh, in fact, I think she wanted it too much.

I'm formulating the impression that one way Mr. G deals with his sense of emotional injury is to avoid looking inward; rather than get in touch with his own failings or inadequacies, he externalizes by focusing on his wife and finding fault with her.

PB: In the beginning of the relationship?

MR. G: Yeah, in the beginning of the relationship. She wanted it, you know, like all the time. It was like a big problem. And I had, uh, worked it out so that we did it like twice a week. And that was comfortable. And, she . . . I don't know, she just got more and more unfriendly. I'd ask her to do things, you know, like give her a job to do while I was at work, things to take care of, things around the house. And, uh, I don't know she didn't seem to get into that kind of thing. And finally, uh, she told me that she was going to leave. She wanted to leave with our daughter.

Mr. G sounds like he has a one-person view of marriage and relationships. He seems to think of his wife as an employee who was not enjoying her job, even though he was a good boss. I wonder what his parents' relationship was like and what, if any, other relationships he has had. What will this hold for our relationship? This has already been hinted at in my experience that he wishes for me to fix him.

PB: How long have you been married?

MR. G: Uh, ten years.

PB: And what was her reason for wanting to leave?

MR. G: Well she didn't really make it clear, but I think she's seeing other guys and I think that's what she wanted. I think she just wanted to go out and have a lot of sex. That's really what I think it was all about. And, uh, what can you do about something like that?

Mr. G seems to experience himself as the victim of his wife's excessive sexual ap-petite and to be asking for my concurrence and support. I'm supposed to get on the bandwagon and blame his wife, too.

PB: Well do . . . was there anything about you that she was unhappy with?

At the time, I was aware of wanting to probe for the extent to which Mr. G was capa-ble of self-examination and insight. How entrenched was his defense of externalization? In retrospect, this is one of those interventions that, while probing for self-awareness, nevertheless has the effect of being injurious and promotes, not insight, but antagonism or opposition.

MR. G: About me? Um . . . about me? No. I don't see why that would be? I mean I was a good husband. I came home. And I came home every night right after work. Every night after work I came home. Uh, I took her to museums . . . occa-sionally. You know . . . she liked to spend money that I was a little bit concerned about. I didn't want to spend as much money as she did. I . . . I don't know? That's what I, I don't understand.

Mr. G seems incredulous ("About me?") that I could be questioning whether his dilemma has anything to do with him. In fact, my intervention seems to have increased his defensiveness. I think now that my intervention made him feel humiliated. He was asking for me to support his externalization, and my intervention undercut him.

PB: So that's the best explanation you can find for yourself? She was . . . that she had these strong sexual feelings for other people?

I continue testing for insight and self-reflective capacity, but the way the comment is formed sounds a bit contemptuous to me now.

MR. G: She had them in general . . . like real strong sexual feelings.

PB: But your feeling was that since they were diminishing for you maybe they were building up towards others?

MR. G: I think so . . . that's right. I'm pretty suspicious of her regarding that.

PB: Why do you think she got less sexually interested in you?

Once again, I'm consciously testing for the potential for self-reflection.

MR. G: I don't know? I just, I just . . . that puzzles me, that really and truly puzzles me that she got so turned off. I tried to talk to her about it but nothing. Nothing whatsoever ever got straightened out.

No evidence of self-awareness or self-reflective curiosity. Mr. G is defending against his feelings, perhaps of hurt or inadequacy, by blaming his wife for his victimized state. My efforts to promote self-examination seem to be making him wary of me, as if he suspects I am finding fault with him.

PB: You mentioned, uh, before that you felt for a long time that people don't like you?

MR. G: No. I . . . it just occurred to me recently that nobody (*laughs*) . . . gets involved with me.

By correcting my observation, Mr. G seems to be getting irritated with me. I have failed to support his defenses and I am threatening his precarious self-organization.

PB: Any thoughts about why that might be?

In retrospect, I sense Mr. G was closing down in the face of my failure to support his externalizations and the criticism that this implied. I seem to be narcissistically injuring him by persisting in my efforts to explore his contributions to his marital problems.

MR. G: No thoughts about that. No.

PB: You just became aware of it the other day?

MR. G: Well, it just sort of popped into my mind today as a matter of fact. It was a funny kind of experience. It's like out of nowhere . . . maybe I can get him to get people to like me? He can help. You know, he can help me with that.

PB: Can you tell me when you first began to feel that people didn't like you? The first . . . looking back on it maybe, when you started to see that people didn't like you?

I'm having that "walking-on-eggshells" feeling. I have to pick my words very carefully to avoid provoking his defensiveness, but that is because I have been injuring Mr. G with my questioning.

MR. G: (*scratching head*) Uh, well . . . you know, uh . . . my um. . . . I don't know, it's like my, my father, uh, my father was always kind of, uh, working all the time, you know what I mean? He was like working all the time. And, he never . . . he never did things with me. Uh, that's one of the things I think about when you ask me that question. You know, my father was always working or always telling me to do things but never getting into things *with* me.

This association sounds like he is identifying his father as an early figure who didn't like him. His associating to historical material is promising.

PB: How did you feel about that?

MR. G: Ah, that was the way it was. That was the way it was in our house. Our father worked, and my mother was sick, and you know I visited my grandparents. 'Cause they were, they were kind of friendly.

Clearly, Mr. G has difficulty recognizing and articulating feelings. He doesn't respond to my question with feelings, but with more externalizations ("That was the way it was").

PB: Maybe you're suggesting that you thought your father didn't like you?

MR. G: He didn't seem to be like enthusiastic about me, and my mother was always like, uh, bitchy, irritable . . . sick.

He shifts the focus onto his mother.

PB: Sick?

MR. G: Sick, yeah. Sick, sick, sick.

PB: Can you tell me, uh, about what she had, what illness or? . . .

MR. G: Yeah, she had a serious problem with her colon. And when I was about . . . oh I was about thirteen she, uh, she had this major operation. And they took out, you know, her colon. And, uh, and she was always like . . . ever since then she was always like, uh, irritable.

PB: Since the operation?

MR. G: Yeah, since the operation.

PB: Was she sick long before that?

MR. G: Yeah, seems like it. Seems like it . . . all these trips to the hospital and, you know, things like that, going to see doctors all the time.

PB: And as a young child was, uh, she healthier?

MR. G: I don't remember. She always seemed to be irritable. That's all I can think of at the moment, that she was irritable. And, you know, giving orders and, uh, things like that.

Another promising association, but lacking affect.

PB: Do you have siblings?

MR. G: Siblings? Uh, yeah, yeah, you mean like brothers and sisters?

PB: Brothers and sisters.

MR. G: Yeah, uh, well I have, uh, I have two sisters, and I have three brothers.

PB: And where did you come?

MR. G: Where did I come? I'm number two. I'm the second oldest, and I'm the oldest boy.

PB: And what's your relationship with your brothers and sisters?

MR. G: Well, I lived with one of my brothers for a long time. We had a co-op . . . out in Brooklyn for a long time. And we get along fairly well. Uh (*laughs*), you know . . . you know what I mean? Get together occasionally. Get together and maybe talk a little bit but that's about it.

PB: How old are you now?

MR. G: Forty-nine.

PB: And you've been married about ten years?

MR. G: Yep.

PB: Were you married previously?

MR. G: No, I wasn't . . . had a lot of girlfriends. Uh, you know, had a lot of girl-friends and, uh, but somehow they never really . . . they always sort of drifted away. And, uh, so I lived with my brother, and I had these girlfriends. And some-how they just never got, they always got up to a peak and then they just sort of petered out and then next thing you know they'd be gone.

Again, Mr. G presents himself as the innocent victim of a process that is beyond his understanding and control. His nonverbal communications seem to be trying to enlist my sympathy with his plight.

PB: I'm having a little trouble following that. Can you explain that process a lit-tle? What kind of peak would they go from?

In retrospect, I think that saying that I was having a little trouble following his story might feel to him like a negation of his victimhood and, therefore, another injurious comment.

MR. G: Peak? Well, like in the beginning, you know, they would really like me, and I would really like them and we'd be very romantic and we would go do things together. And, it would be very, uh, you know there'd be a lot of hugging, and I would think about her a lot. And then, uh, I would live with her. I lived with a number of women. And, uh, and then uh there were just, um, it wouldn't go any place. It would, uh, start to, the women would start to . . . I'm thinking of one I'd lived with for two years in Seattle and, uh, one fine day she told me that she wasn't happy living with me and, uh, turns out she started to have an affair with a buddy of mine. And the next thing you know she had her own apartment, and I was living all by myself so I came back to New York. What can I tell you? That's the way that worked out.

His life is a mystery to him, so I try to make a relatively obvious connection, tying together his prior experience with what has happened to him recently with his wife.

PB: Well, I guess if we include what you suspect about your wife this is another example of a woman being involved with another man while she was with you?

MR. G: Eh, maybe, I don't know. I don't know. I . . . I'm having a hard time understanding it.

Since he seems incapable of insight or self-reflection, I make a process observation that I hope will engage his curiosity. However, for Mr. G, accepting this observation would necessitate the kind of self-examination that would involve some humiliation and shame, affects he works hard to keep out of awareness. This has, indeed, put Mr. G and me at cross-purposes. The more I try to promote insight and self-examination, the more I threaten his fragile self-organization and risk exposing feelings of shame and humiliation that he is organized around warding off. What sane person would want to continue such an interaction that threatens his organization of experience?

PB: It seems like there's a lot about your life that you don't understand so well. Things seem to happen and maybe there's some external reasons for it, but . . . but there's . . . there's a sense that you don't really understand very much why things have happened to you. They just seem to have happened.

Since my previous attempts at probing for insight and self-examination have fallen on defended ears, I now offer a process observation.

MR. G: Well, I'm a . . . I'm a nice guy you know. I mean . . . I really try hard. A lot of people say that about me. They say, you know, I'm basically a nice guy. You know what I mean? They say I'm a very nice guy. And I get along with people . . . and I try hard. You know? Just the way it is . . . I mean that's the kind of stuff . . . you know what I mean?

PB: That's circumstance? That's life?

I think that I am ironically highlighting his defense of externalization.

MR. G: Uh . . .yeah, something like that. You know what I mean?

Mr. G has detected some hostility and some threat to his organization of experience in my ironic tone, and his tone becomes irritable and challenging.

PB: I guess when, when you first came in you, you said you had a fleeting thought that maybe I could help you so that people would like you. I guess that suggested that maybe you felt that there was something about you that could change . . . that would make your relationships with people different.

I spell it out as clearly as I can, that therapy is about him and not about our agreeing that the world and women have treated him unfairly.

MR. G: Me change? Uh . . . gee, I never thought about it as me changing. I kind of thought about you, um, sort of, uh, I guess doing something so that people would like me. You know, that you would.

PB: Have you ever thought about what that was I might do?

I am incredulous and my question is provocative.

MR. G: Well, I just thought, you know, you're a psychologist. You have a doctorate. I thought, you know, you'd have a lot of things to tell me, uh, that would make me, uh, maybe more interesting. You know what I mean? Things like that.

He says this with quite a bit of disdain. He is clearly getting irritated with me.

PB: Is there some feeling that maybe you're not interesting enough?

MR. G: Well, it's beginning to look that way. I mean, I have to, you know, begin to kind of come to that conclusion. That's, uh, I hate to admit it but . . . boy do I hate to admit that.

PB: Why is that hard for you?

Another attempt to direct his attention to his internal experience. Not surprisingly, it is more acceptable for Mr. G to feel "uninteresting" than to consider that there might be something more troubled about him.

MR. G: Oh shit, man, how would you like to be forty-nine years old and come to the realization that you're not interesting? And you have to go see a doctor to help you get interesting. I mean that's not a . . . you know what I mean? Understand? Right?

Said with utter contempt for me. Clearly, there was a great personal cost for him to have to acknowledge that he was not interesting. He seems to feel I badgered him into this admission and is now resentful. For both of us, this is the culmination of our struggle, which has not left either of us feeling very good about our encounter.

PB: I guess, I guess your feeling is then that you're a pretty nice guy but not an interesting one?

Hearing myself say these words, I become aware that I have been feeling increasingly annoyed by Mr. G's externalizing defenses and his expressions of contempt for my noble attempts to promote insight. I have retaliated by making a statement that, to my ears, sounds smug and sarcastic. This was the low point of the session for me, but also, surprisingly the turning point.

MR. G: I'm, I'm, I . . . you know, it's sad to say I think you're, uh, I think that's, uh . . . I think you're right about that.

I am shocked into my senses by this response. Even though the words may not read so strongly, I heard myself make an exasperated, hostile comment, and Mr. G reacted as if what I said was somehow attuned. It suddenly comes to me that my attempts to promote insight and self-awareness have threatened his organization of experience and increased his defensiveness. I have been injuring him by pushing for insights that could only be experienced by him as shameful and humiliating admissions. He is defending against my analytic stance, which he seems to experience as deeply threatening and humiliating. In an instant, I realize that I can change the intersubjective field we have co-constructed by adopting an empathically attuned stance in which I relate to his subjective affective states in a more attuned, sensitive manner. If I am successful, he might feel less threatened, respond less defensively, and become more accessible to our relationship.

PB: Do you feel that people haven't appreciated how nice you are?

I say this with an affirming tone that I hope conveys that I accept that he is a nice guy who has been misunderstood by a cold world.

MR. G: Well, you know, I think that might be. I think that just might be. I mean I *really* try hard. I'm a very good guy in a lot of ways. You know I try very hard. I get along. I call people up. I go to their house. I take, you know, the women I've been involved with, I remember when I was younger, I was always willing to take them for a ride. I was always willing to do lots of different things with them. And, geez, sooner or later they'd slip, slip away . . . get married to somebody else. I was in the Merchant Marine for a year, and when I came back (*claps his hands together to suggest the suddenness and unexpectedness of this development*) my girlfriend . . . married. How do you like that? You know what I mean?

This is a remarkable flow of material. As we said before (Buirski and Haglund 2001), when you accurately articulate the patient's subjective experience, the patient has lots to say. Accurately attuned articulations promote the flow of associations. The whole tone of the session has changed. We are now allies in the process. Earlier in the session, when I challenged his pleas for sympathy by directing the focus onto his contributions to those situations, he would become more defensive and less forthcoming.

PB: You had hoped she'd wait around.

MR. G: She was my girlfriend. I was off at sea making money. You know what I mean? Why, why shouldn't she wait for me?

PB: Well, I guess the things that you're describing about yourself in relationships, particularly to women, it sounds like you, you try to do the right thing and you try to treat them well but that they seem to be reacting as if there's something *else* that they may be missing in their involvement with you?

I was doing well, but this reflects a bit of a relapse. Here, I am trying to make connections instead of remaining attuned to his experience. I fear I have injured him and instigated renewed defensiveness.

MR. G: The other side of the coin that occurs to me from time to time is that, I know this sounds a little bit, uh, unpleasant, but it's like sometimes I get the feeling that women are bitches. That's another thought I had about this. That they're just bitches, period. You know what I mean?

It is interesting, but not surprising, that when injured, he resurrects his externalizing defenses. While this is a major defense in his repertoire, it is instructive that it comes into play only in reaction to my injurious interventions. This is a demonstration of the workings of the intersubjective system. When he experiences me as attuned and validating, he is able to associate more freely and be more open and self-reflective. When I make connections or interpretations, he feels threatened and his defenses become mobilized.

PB: Oh! Tell me more about this.

I am uncritically curious and wish to know more. I felt like I understood how hurtful his experiences with his mother and other women have been and I try to communicate my acceptance of his feeling state.

MR. G: Eh . . . just, just uh, bitches. I mean that's the word that comes to mind you know what I mean? Bitchy, bitchy, bitchy, bitchy. You know . . . want this, want that, want this, want that. You know what I mean? Irritable, irritable, irritable. You can't give them enough. You can't give them. . . .

PB: Can't give them enough!

I say this with a noncritical tone of acceptance of his subjective experience with women. I am accepting his experience that the women in his life have been bitchy to him, not that I am agreeing that women are bitches.

MR. G: (*emphasizing every word*) Can't give them enough. I mean I gave it to her twice a week. You know what I mean? **Twice a week** I gave it to her! (*irri-*

tated) And you'd think she'd be happy with that but, no, she was always kind of hanging around looking like she was kind of wanting something. You know what I mean? I was busy. I had things to do. I had my career.

PB: So as much as you felt you were giving there was still a feeling that they were acting as if you weren't giving enough? They wanted more?

I really understood that from his world of affective experience, he has always felt treated as deficient and inadequate. He needs to experience that I understand this, uncritically and without negative judgment.

MR. G: Yes!

He emphatically confirms that I got it right.

PB: They weren't satisfied with what you were giving?

I'm trying to put myself in his shoes.

MR. G: That's right. That's right. I worked! I worked, worked, worked, worked, worked!

Again, he emphatically affirms that I got his experience right.

PB: You were never really appreciated?

I keep at it.

MR. G: I went to school at night; worked during the day.

PB: Sounds like it! It sounds like you really worked very hard and have felt that you weren't appreciated?

I affirm his subjective experience and I continue articulating his feeling that he has never been appreciated. I am providing mirroring selfobject functions that, over time, will hopefully enable him to integrate his affective experience, shore up his flagging self-esteem and promote self-cohesion.

MR. G: Well, that's, that's there's something to that I'll tell you right now . . . yeah!

More confirmation from him. We are really on the same page now.

PB: Certainly sounds like you felt you weren't appreciated by your wife and, uh, how about the other women in your life too? . . . How about your mother? You mentioned that, that she's irritable, that she was irritable.

I risk making an interpretive connection, but I'm counting on his experience of me as noncritical, attuned, and accepting of his experience.

MR. G: Yeah!

How quickly the intersubjective field has shifted. Instead of an externalization, he offers a strong affirmation. It gives me confidence to proceed.

PB: Do you think she appreciated you?

MR. G: Uh . . . no, no. I think my mother in some ways is anti-male. That's a thought I've had over the years, you know, that she's, uh, there's a quality about her, the castrating bitch. You know, you've heard that expression? I heard that expression. Eh, so she always sort of put my father down and **he** never did enough. **He** never worked enough. You know, nag, nag, nag. That kind of, uh, attitude.

This no longer sounds like an externalizing defense. Now it sounds like a description of the interpersonal environment in which his experience of himself as a man and his experience of women had become organized.

PB: And did she treat you that way too?

MR. G: Uh, you know, yeah, kind of yeah . . . she was much more friendly with the girls than she was with me . . . and the other guys, the other boys. Yeah, that's, that's the way my mother was. That's the way she still is! She was always checking up on my girlfriends, too, you know what I mean? I mean I'd bring a girlfriend around the next thing you know she didn't like her! She had some complaint about her! You know, it always seemed to happen that way. She was always complaining about the girlfriends I brought around. She didn't like my wife! You know what I mean, she was always complaining. Criticizing! Criticizing!

PB: So, you didn't feel that she appreciated you very much. Did you feel . . . was she affectionate with you?

I continue to articulate the organizing principle of not feeling appreciated. As I immerse myself in the empathic-introspective stance, I am trying to put myself into his experiential world. I find myself feeling warmly toward Mr. G and I sense that his world had very little affection in it. His life, I imagine, must have felt very cold, isolated, and unloving. Of course, this should have been obvious since he came to me as a result of having been left by his wife, but I now feel the absence of a loving presence in his life very strongly and I share this impression with him.

MR. G: No! No! I can, uh, **never** remember her being affectionate now that you ask that question. She was always worried about this, or irritable about that.

We have created a safer relational environment in which he can reveal himself without the fear that I will narcissistically injure him.

PB: So who **was** affectionate with you?

I sense he experiences me as being on his side, meaning he feels safe, understood, and liked.

MR. G: My grandparents! Yeah, my grandfather was particularly, uh, nice to me. I used to visit with him a lot because of that. He used to be a seaman as a matter of fact! He spent many, many years on the sea! He'd tell me all his stories about his years on the sea.

PB: So, uh, you knew him after he gave up, uh, his sailing days?

MR. G: Oh yeah! I was still a kid, you know. I'd go visit him, go on the subway and go visit him.

PB: And what would he do with you?

MR. G: I didn't hear.

PB: What would he do with you? What was your experience with him like?

MR. G: I don't know. He just, uh, he got a big smile! He got a big smile on his face when I would, uh . . . (*looking up at ceiling, eyes welling up with tears, getting choked up*).

PB: Seems like you had a, uh, pain then?

I try to gently and supportively observe his emotional reaction. We are clearly on new affective terrain.

MR. G: Yeah, you know . . .

He is choked up, wiping away his tears. Long pause.

PB: You miss him.

I try to put his affective experience into words.

MR. G: Yeah! (*long pause*)

PB: When did you last see him?

MR. G: (*pause*) I don't know? He died when I was in my middle thirties I think?

PB: He was the major person whom you felt close with.

I let a minute or so of silence pass. This is a working silence. Mr. G seems to be immersed in feelings that have formerly been warded off.

PB: You seem moved when you think about it.

MR. G: Yeah. (*a long silence*)

PB: Is that an experience you often have?

MR. G: No. (*silence*)

PB: You don't usually feel these kinds of feelings.

MR. G: No. (*downcast look, staring at floor*) Doesn't feel good. Feels like I'm coming apart around in here, you know (*pointing to heart, wiping tears*). *About ten more seconds of silence.*

MR. G: Well, what else do you want to know?

For Mr. G, feelings are disorganizing and disruptive, and he attempts to move away, usually by externalization or other distancing maneuvers. I venture an observation of the process.

PB: It would be easier to move onto something else and, uh, skip with that.

MR. G: Mmm.

PB: Has there been anyone else who's moved you in the same way?

I would like to stay with these affects, but I don't want to force the issue in the first session. I offer an opportunity for displacement—keep on the same affect but switch the object.

MR. G: (*sigh . . . silence three–four seconds*) I don't know?

PB: Did you work hard to please him, too?

Since Mr. G is having difficulty associating, I ask a question to which we both now know the answer. It might have been preferable to articulate this as a statement, ("He was someone you didn't have to work hard to please") not a question, as I wish to convey that I understand his experience.

MR. G: No. I didn't have to please him.

PB: Didn't have to do that.

I offer reflective affirmation of his comment.

MR. G: Just come to his house and that was all I had to do.

PB: Hasn't been so easy with everybody else.

I say this as an observation, not a question.

MR. G: Guess not. (*silence . . . eight–nine seconds; looking at ceiling, crying*)

PB: It seems like you really let yourself get in touch with some very painful feelings that you don't often allow yourself to have.

I make an observation about the therapy process, not at all confident that this is a process that he will want to engage in further.

MR. G: Yeah, I miss, I miss him. Didn't even know I miss him.

PB: You haven't thought about him in a while.

MR. G: Sort of, didn't think about him, you know? (*Mr. G unbuttons his vest, as if to relieve a feeling of constriction . . . mumbles.*) My tie's a little tight. (*loosens tie, finishes unbuttoning his vest*)

PB: Do you think there's any similar feeling of missing involved in your feelings toward your wife?

Making this connection seems a bit rushed. I don't have to complete most of his treatment in the first session. But, I wanted Mr. G to have a sense of how the therapy process can proceed; that rather than fix him, together, we can make sense of his life experience.

MR. G: Uh, yeah, I guess?

PB: There was a time when she was affectionate with you?

MR. G: Yeah.

PB: So maybe this has been a really painful experience?

MR. G: I'm just now understanding it. I never knew I missed her. Still feel she's a bitch all the same. Could punch her (*forms fist*) . . . right in the . . .

PB: Angry that she's hurt you this way.

I try to make his anger more understandable by connecting it to his painful feelings of injury. (Mr. G leans head back and covers his eyes.)

MR. G: (*looks at watch*) What time is it? How much time . . . how much? When are . . . uh. (*wiping eyes*)

PB: We have about, uh, five minutes left.

MR. G: So what are we gonna do? How are we gonna work? What's gonna happen here, you know? (*he picks lint off his pants, as if disinterested*)

PB: Well, if we do work together, one of the things that may happen is that you may begin to experience the kind of uncomfortable feelings you're feeling now, more often. (*Mr. G wipes his tears away*) It seems to me that maybe you've worked hard to not let yourself feel hurt? That maybe you felt hurt ever since you were very little. And . . . that you've worked hard to act well, to be good to people, be nice to people, but not to let yourself feel that too much. And one of the things that may happen is you may start to feel those feelings more? Maybe you'll start to feel a lot of feelings, a lot of different feelings more? And maybe that will be kind of scary? (*Mr. G looks at floor, wipes eyes, looks at the ceiling*)

My intention with this rambling articulation was to anticipate any wish of Mr. G's to avoid the surfacing of further painful feelings. By putting his avoidant wishes into words, I hoped to forestall a flight from treatment.

MR. G: Yeah, yeah okay now let me figure this out now. You're gonna . . . what's gonna happen here between you and me? I mean what's the idea? I come to see you? How much, what . . . how much is it gonna cost me?

While Mr. G seems to want to continue seeing me, I fear that too much has been surfaced too quickly and that now the issue of fees will provide him a rationale to discontinue.

PB: Well, um, we'll . . . we'll get to that in a second. I guess I'm having the sense that the things we're talking about have been painful (*Mr. G gets his calendar out of his briefcase*), and I'm not sure that you'll want to go through more sessions where you might have painful feelings?

I realize that I am now speaking from a one-person objectivist stance, about him and his resistances, rather than being attuned to his experience. We have shared a "moment of meeting" (Stern et al. 1998) and, in retrospect, my fear of his flight from treatment seems exaggerated.

MR. G: (*irritated*) I don't know why we're talking about this now? I want to know how much, uh, how much am I going to pay for this? I mean, you know? You know, what's, what's, that's what I want to know. I want you to tell me those things.

I hear Mr. G saying that he wants me to care for him, guide him, perhaps in ways no one has before. This brings me back to thinking intersubjectively.

MR. G: You know, I'm kind of thinking time is almost up. I'm almost positive that time is up. I'm thinking that, uh, I kind of have a feeling that we should get straightened out for whether we're gonna work together 'cause I know people come to see therapists, you know, quite a few times. And, uh, I got . . . I've got an appointment. (*holding up calendar, smiling in a friendly way*) You know, I've got a busy schedule. I really do!

I hear Mr. G asking for recognition that he is a busy, important man who seeks respect and reciprocal engagement.

PB: Okay . . . then, then let's sort of look at it this way. When you first came in, uh, you talked about people, wondering if people liked you, that you had that thought today, that people don't like you. (*Mr. G starts scratching his head*) I guess I'm wondering how you feel I feel about you?

This was an attempt to get away from my previous focus on the potential for Mr. G to use fear of pain or fees as a resistance to continuing treatment, and, instead, to engage him on a relational level.

MR. G: (*confused*) How you feel about me? Well, I'm getting anxious that you don't want to see me anymore! (*drops calendar at side of chair*) I'm beginning to feel that. . . . We keeping talking about it's gonna be painful, and you don't know if I can take the pain! (*sits up and begins to button jacket*)

PB: You feel like I may not want to work with you.

Here I am trying to put words to his fear of rejection. Mr. G has interpreted my efforts to explore his potential resistance as an indication that I don't want to work with him. Fortunately, by my articulating his fears, Mr. G feels understood and freer to risk revealing himself. I am wondering whether he dreads that I will turn out to be like the women in his life.

MR. G: I'm wondering . . . yeah . . . yeah! Well, if you don't . . . you know, I'm, I'm not sure that you like me? I mean I get that feeling, I guess, something like that. I mean I want to get this thing straightened out, and get set and get going in terms of a schedule. I mean I, I need to make that straightened out. I need to work this thing out with regard to my budget. And, uh . . . (*laughs*) . . . you seem like a, there's something about you that I like! I will say that! You have a nice quality.

I feel very touched by this flow of associations. Mr. G has started with his typical focus on the external, but suddenly caught himself and, for the first time, risking some self-reflective capacity, looks at his own feelings. I sense that Mr. G is feeling safe with me, and I am feeling warmly toward him. I think that this is a good example of how insight and the deepening of self-awareness can come about through the empathic/introspective stance and not just the interpretive stance.

PB: What is that? What is that?

MR. G: Uh . . . I think there's sort of a quality about you. You have a nice friendly quality. I like that.

PB: Well, okay, uh . . . if you feel that way, we can work together. I would certainly be willing and interested to work with you.

I want to affirm that indeed something warm and friendly has occurred between us and that I do, in fact, want to work with him. This is a mirroring and affirming intervention, and I anticipate that it will make Mr. G feel good about our working together.

MR. G: I'm glad to hear that!

PB: And I would suggest that we meet, uh, twice a week.

Usually I would not bring up frequency in the first session with someone whom I thought was wary of engaging in the therapy process. However, those earlier concerns of mine have been reduced by Mr. G's mirroring of me. Clearly, Mr. G and I have been engaged in a process of self and mutual regulation. Now I feel confident that Mr. G will experience my recommendation as confirming my desire to work with him.

MR. G: Mm, boy, twice a week! Wow! With my schedule twice a week?

PB: What did you have in mind when you called? Did you have an expectation?

MR. G: Wow, twice a week huh? Well I was thinking more like once a week? But you know it's so funny when you said twice a week it, uh, made me feel good. It's like, uh, like you want to see me more, more often you know what I mean? And it's nice! But, then on the other hand how much is that going to cost me you know? . . .

PB: Right.

MR. G: Twice a week. A psychologist, what do you charge you know?

PB: My fee is X dollars a session *(the going rate at the time).*

MR. G: Whew! Boy! X dollars a session! *(rubs forehead)* Wow, 2X dollars a week! That's how many times? Times four that's 8X dollars a month! *(whistles)* That's a lot of money!

PB: It is.

MR. G: But, uh . . . well, that's a lot of money.

PB: Do you feel you can afford it?

MR. G: Well, I have to take a look at my budget and, uh you know, work on that. I know I have insurance where I work. As a matter of fact, I've been told that it's pretty good now that I think about it. Uh, I'll check that out and see what the situation is in regard to that.

PB: Mmhmm.

MR. G: You know, I got a lot of expenses, child support and, uh, I don't want to tell you. You know how cost of living is these days.

PB: What, what did you expect it would cost?

MR. G: Oh, I don't know. Gee, uh, maybe 3X or 4X dollars? I didn't, I didn't know. I just wasn't thinking about that too much. It just popped into my mind here a little while back. How much is it going to cost and, eh, that sort of thing. (*silence . . . two seconds*) 'Cause, you know, you were so friendly I was getting a little suspicious like you were, you were trying to be friendly but you really wanted to, you know, get the old bucks, something like that. That's, you know, came to my mind.

PB: That, that in a way maybe I would try to get you to do for me like you do then for everybody else?

In retrospect, I would prefer to have made a clearer articulation that would capture his fear that I might be manipulating and exploiting him. I would have preferred to say, "You've had the experience of people taking advantage of your good intentions and you worry maybe I am just like them."

MR. G: You were gonna be friendly and then get money from me.

PB: Uh-huh.

MR. G: That's what I felt.

PB: Well, I'm glad you could say that. Well? Um. How would you like to leave things? Would you like to make an appointment for another session and think about it for a few days and come back and we'll discuss it further?

MR. G: Okay. Yeah . . . yeah. Sounds like a good idea.

PB: Good. Then . . . let's meet on Thursday.

MR. G: Wait just a minute! (*smiling, picks up calendar*) Hold on then! (*said lightly, with humor*)

Mr. G wants me to respect that he is a busy person and that I should not take him for granted. We will be meeting on equal ground.

PB: Okay.

MR. G: Thursday, uh, this coming Thursday. Today is Tuesday. Thursday . . . let's see, Thursday what time did you want to meet?

PB: When have you got free?

Here I wanted to convey that I do respect him and his schedule. This relationship will be more mutual than most for him—he will have a voice and be heard.

MR. G: Let's see, I'm looking at the schedule here . . . we're talking April 25th, right, Doc? Okay, April 25th? Let's see, well what . . . April 25th that's a Thursday. I work, I work nine to . . . uh, I get off at five I could be here at six.

PB: Let's see, I have a 6:30 and a, uh, 8:00 time free.

Since I have both times free, I want to give him the choice.

MR. G: 6:30.

PB: 6:30? Okay.

MR. G: Okay. Let me just write that down. (*again with some lightness and humor*) And then I'll talk over the money situation with you then okay?

PB: Right. Okay.

Intersubjective systems theory, consistent with the work on dynamic systems (Stolorow 1997; Thelen and Smith 1994) predicts that any perturbation to the system will have an effect on the entire system. By my changing my engagement stance, Mr. G necessarily must change as well. In contrast to isolated-mind perspectives that treat the individual as a fixed, static unit, intersubjective systems theory recognizes the complex interplay of forces in shaping the field.

In this session transcript, I have tried to show how a shift in the therapist's approach to the relationship instigates a corresponding shift in the relational style of the other. Whether I performed well in my two stances, as a practitioner of structural theory or in practicing intersubjectively, I think the clinical material reveals that the theory of the therapist informs the practice and the way practice is performed shapes the nature and quality of the therapeutic engagement. In this example, Mr. G became more sullen and resistant when approached from an insight-oriented perspective that he seems to experience as narcissistically injurious. He became increasingly irritable and disparaging of the therapist. We might say that Mr. G appeared to be showing characteristics of borderline personality organization. When engaged from a stance that attuned to, mirrored, and affirmed his affective experience, Mr. G became more open to feelings and self-reflective about his experience and the meanings he made of that experience. He presented in a decidedly nonborderline manner and, in fact, seemed quite vulnerable and sensitive. Clearly, the way Mr. G related to his therapist was very much influenced and shaped by the way his therapist interacted and engaged with him.

We have traditionally been led to expect that insight results from interpreting resistance and defense against knowing. In contrast, here is an illustration of how the empathic/introspective stance, with its focus on attunement to affect states, furthers self-reflection through avoidance of interactions that provoke defensiveness. Rather than defenses operating to prevent unconscious knowledge from entering consciousness, defensiveness is seen as a self-protective attempt to ward off injurious interactions. Mr. G, who at first appears to be a poor candidate for insight-oriented therapy, turns out to be quite open to knowing and revealing his inner affect states.

Chapter Four

Colliding Worlds of Experience

As Stolorow, Atwood, and Orange (2002) have observed, "An intersubjective field, the central theoretical construct of intersubjectivity theory, is defined as a system composed of differently organized, interacting subjective worlds" (p. 33). They go on to describe how "the experiential world seems to be both inhabited by and inhabiting of the human being. People live in worlds, and worlds in people" (p. 34). A person's worlds of experience include the impact of culture and the norms and values that the culture supports (see chapter 5 for a further discussion of the impact of culture), the person's developmental and family history, and the beliefs and value systems instilled there.

For therapists, their worlds of experience include the history and philosophy of their training, especially their theory of mind, and the beliefs and values rooted within that system. In chapters 2 and 3, I have focused on one aspect of the therapist's worlds of experience, the therapist's theory of mind, where I tried to show how this shaped and influenced the therapeutic process for both Miss K and Mr. G. In this chapter, I want to focus on another side of the intersubjective field—the worlds of experience that people bring to their relationship with their therapists and the conflicts that emerge when these two worlds of experience collide.

When Freud first introduced his theories on the workings of the mind, he was met with skepticism and sometimes outright derision. However, by the time of his death, psychoanalytic thinking was already exerting a powerful influence on Western thought. As W. H. Auden (1940) wrote in his poem, " In Memory of Sigmund Freud,"

> if often he was wrong and, at times, absurd,
> to us he is no more a person
> now but a whole climate of opinion

And Peter Gay (1989), the noted historian, has observed, "Sigmund Freud—along with Karl Marx, Charles Darwin, and Albert Einstein—is among that small handful of supreme makers of the twentieth-century mind whose works should be our prized possession" (p. xi). Through the end of the twentieth century, cultural criticism, whether of the literary or performing arts, and social and political commentary were deeply informed by Freudian thinking.

In recent times, some of Freud's most cherished ideas, like the death instinct, the universality of the Oedipus complex, and penis envy, have come under intense criticism, much like the criticism Freud experienced in his early days. Ironically, one important legacy of Freud's work has been the way other of his most important concepts have been so seamlessly woven into the fabric of Western cultural consciousness that they are experienced by most people as self-evident truths, part of the collective wisdom of the culture. Because these ideas have become so embedded in the collective cultural consciousness, they are no longer even seen as associated with Freud. Even those who reject much of Freudian theory nevertheless unknowingly accept these Freudian ideas as givens. Such ideas as finding meaning in other people's slips of the tongue, the power and influence of unconscious motivation, the formative nature of childhood experience in shaping adult personality, and the tendency for people who are in the grip of conflict to repeat their earlier relational patterns are just some of the examples of the infiltration of Freudian ideas into the collective cultural consciousness. For example, most people dismiss their own Freudian slips as being psychologically meaningless, but enjoy finding meaning when someone else makes a slip. If a man calls his girlfriend by the name of another woman, he might dismiss it as meaningless, but his girlfriend will likely reveal herself to have assimilated Freudian ideas. Mary may not be amused when referred to as Jane. "Who is Jane?" she is likely to ask, thereby attributing unconscious meaning to the error.

As Freud's painful personal experience demonstrates, it took a very long time for developments in psychoanalytic thinking to permeate the cultural landscape. Once embedded, though, it has taken an equally long time for new ideas to replace them. For example, much has been written in the professional literature about the debate between one-person versus two-person psychologies. These ideas have been in the analytic literature for twenty-five years, and all analytically oriented therapists have grappled with them. But such ideas have not yet found their way into the collective cultural consciousness.

Ideas about the subjective nature of reality, the relativity of meaning and truth, mutual influence, and the contextual construction of experience, though familiar to analysts, philosophers, and students of postmodernism, are by no means familiar to the general public. What this means is that people who come to therapy today often bring with them some embedded version of an older psychoanalytic vision of how their minds operate. These older belief systems of how the mind operates influence the meaning that people then make of their experience. As psychologists have long known, belief systems, particularly beliefs about oneself and one's motives, are especially difficult to modify. The implication for treatment is that for those seeking psychotherapy today, their worlds of experience have been shaped by a twentieth-century view of the psychological landscape and they often find their views colliding with the differing worlds of experience of twenty-first-century psychotherapists. Put in the language of intersubjective systems theory, people come to therapy with an isolated-mind view of their mental functioning and they are frequently encountering therapists who hold a relational and contextualist perspective. Reconciling the divergent worlds of experience of these two participants in the therapy process poses both a challenge to the therapeutic relationship and an opportunity for growth and transformation.

In traditional one-person treatments, when the worlds of experience of the two members of the therapy dyad collide, the therapist's vision was typically presumed to be true and accurate. If the patient didn't accept the therapist's vision, he or she might, in the traditional sense, be thought to be resisting. The traditional psychoanalytic notion of resistance viewed people as needing to defend against the displeasure aroused by new insight into their forbidden desires. From this perspective, people were considered to be resistant to therapy when they warded off, rejected, or thwarted the interpretive efforts of the therapist who was working to promote insight and strengthen the ego. Contemporary Freudians no longer see resistance in terms of the patient's opposition to the therapist. Resistance is now seen as another way that people's problems reveal themselves in therapy. However, even though contemporary analysts, like Adler and Bachant (1998), discuss resistance in more relational and systemic terms, they still utilize the traditional term "resistance," which is burdened with the weight of its historical meanings. "Resistance" is one of those psychoanalytic constructs whose meaning is changing even though the same term is used. This produces confusion because concepts like resistance, transference resistance, and the analysis of resistance are nonetheless steeped in isolated-mind theorizing, despite the recognition of the importance of relationships and systems.

I have taken this digression to discuss resistance because I want to emphasize the point that "colliding worlds of experience" is not to be confused with even contemporary versions of "resistance." From the intersubjective systems perspective, one of the interesting challenges facing the participants in the therapy dyad is not overcoming the traditional resistances to insight and knowing but appreciating the tenacity with which people cling to their organizations of experience, the meanings they have made of themselves in the world. The desire to maintain one's organization of experience in the face of a different vision offered by the therapist might look like one of the typical manifestations of resistance. However, as I will try to illustrate, traditional and contemporary notions of resistance do not capture the intersubjective nature of this phenomenon. It is not resistance, in even the modern view of the term, but a collision between differing worlds of experience, negotiated through dialogue, that can lead to the co-construction of new meanings.

As Atwood and Stolorow (1984) have discussed, "The need to maintain the organization of experience is a central motive in the patterning of human action" (p. 35). Experience, as has been illustrated throughout this book, is organized within relational contexts, and personal meanings are very much influenced by the impact of the prevailing culture on the self-organization. As therapists, we know how difficult it is for people to change, to develop new ways of organizing their experience, and how tenaciously people cling to their familiar ways of making sense of their worlds.

When therapists practicing from the intersubjective systems perspective speak of people striving to maintain their invariant organizations of experience, we are describing a motive that is clearly not resistance in any familiar sense of the term. Rather than defending against the knowledge of unacceptable unconscious longings, the desire to maintain the organization of experience persists because to think otherwise defies a lifetime of painful experience from which incontrovertible meanings have been made. People's organizing principles are forged in the heat of formative developmental relationships and they cannot conceive that other meanings could be made of these formative experiences. The very idea is disruptive and destabilizing, especially to vulnerable and tenuous self-organizations. What some might consider to be resistance to the therapeutic efforts of the analyst, the intersubjective systems perspective views as inevitable collisions between differing worlds of experience. The collision is not between one isolated mind resisting the efforts of another isolated mind to uncover hidden longings. The collision is between different worlds of experience and the meanings made from that experience. The first is over mental contents; the second is over meanings and experience. These reflect two entirely different understandings of relational process.

Contemporary relational and intersubjective systems therapists regularly encounter, in the consulting room, people whose organizations of experience have been shaped by the isolated-mind perspective that dominates in the context of Western culture. To these people, inner convictions about themselves carry the certainty of self-evident truths. In effect, many of us find ourselves in the interesting position of being therapists with a contextualist worldview working with people whose worlds of experience are organized around one-person, isolated-mind convictions. This collision is not the traditional one, between the neutral analyst and the infantile developmental conflicts of the patient, but between two people with differing worlds of experience trying to make sense together, to open up possibilities for new ways of organizing experience.

Stolorow, Atwood, and Trop (1992) introduced the idea of intersubjective disjunction to describe one type of therapeutic impasse in which "the therapist assimilates the material expressed by the patient into configurations that significantly alter its meaning for the patient" (p. 103). Intersubjective disjunctions refer then to the kind of power struggles and misunderstandings that intrude when two people with opposing organizing principles try to negotiate their relationship. It refers to interactions that construct an impasse in the therapeutic relationship. The notion of colliding worlds of experience differs from intersubjective disjunction by addressing the differing worldviews and theories of mind that emerge from members of different philosophical and cultural communities. Like political liberals and conservatives, adherence to isolated-mind or contextualist visions of the world leads to the making of personal meanings that seem incomprehensible to the other. Colliding worlds signifies a class of interactions that promote transformation and growth. Such collisions typically occur when the person's view of him- or herself as sick, self-destructive, deeply flawed, and undeserving are depathologized by the therapist, whose view is that these traits reflect the person's striving for health. Like "moments of meeting" (Stern et al. 1998), collisions of worldviews are authentic relational engagements that promote the formation of new organizations of experience, new ways of understanding oneself in the world.

I would like to offer some vignettes from a therapy relationship to illustrate this collision of worlds of experience between the two participants. The areas around which the two collide are quite typical of therapeutic engagements and, far from representing a technical problem that must be solved, it is the fertile ground from which transformation and growth can emerge.

Tracie, a young woman in her late twenties, came to treatment because she was torn over whether to end her engagement. She found out that her fiancé was stealing money from her to support a costly gambling habit. He had agreed to go to Gamblers Anonymous and to couples' therapy. However, in couples' therapy, he blamed Tracie for being withholding and used this to explain his stealing. He attributed his gambling to a need for excitement that he felt was missing in the relationship. He tried to persuade the couples' therapist that Tracie was the cause of his problems. As we will see, Tracie was primed by her developmental experience to accept such blame as plausible. Her dilemma was that if his actions were her fault, then she could save the relationship by going into individual treatment and becoming a better person. On the other hand, perhaps he was a dishonest addict whom she should leave.

Tracie's low sense of self-worth made it hard for her to sort out her contribution to the relationship problems, so Tracie sought out individual therapy. As part of her presenting problem, Tracie reported to her male therapist, "I always choose emotionally unavailable men." What is the therapist to make of this statement? If we unpack Tracie's formulation of her personal dynamic, we find that it contains within it many philosophical and theoretical assumptions and hypotheses about her worlds of experience. Also, even at this early stage, it is likely that the therapist's theoretical worldview and the expectations that derive from it will exert an important influence in shaping the inquiry and explorations that follow. And the therapist's worldview may very well be at variance with the worldview that Tracie carries with her and around which her experience has become organized. Such differing worldviews may become a source of conflict within the therapy relationship. When two worldviews collide, it would be the height of isolated mindedness for one to presume some privileged knowledge of the truth and assume that the other was resisting. The fate of such collisions is always open to question. In all likelihood, both will wind up learning about themselves through their encounter.

Let's examine the implications for the therapeutic process that arise when Tracie and her therapist come to the therapy relationship with differing worldviews. From the outset, a therapist with an intersubjective systems sensibility accepts the subjective validity of Tracie's experience. Tracie appears to hold a set of complex meaningful assumptions about herself and of her interpersonal relationships. Her theory of mind has at least four interconnecting assumptions that together shape her organization of experience and the meanings she has made of it. Each component of Tracie's worldview affects the personal meanings she has made of her experience and will influence the meanings that she and her therapist will be able to make of her experiential worlds.

First, Tracie hypothesized that there was some dynamic or motive in her psychological makeup that caused her to deliberately select men who were emotionally unavailable ("I always choose . . ."). Second, there was the implication that this dynamic that caused her to be attracted to emotionally unavailable men and less drawn to, or avoidant of, more related men, probably operated unconsciously. Third, Tracie seemed to have identified what she considers to be a repetitive pattern in her relating ("I always . . ."). Thus, Tracie seemed to be postulating that she was behaving under the sway of a powerful unconscious force that was characterized by its repetitive quality: that she was in the grip of some need to repeat. And fourth, her failure to prevent this repetitive pattern from occurring reflected some fundamental flaw in her psychological makeup that doomed her to be forever disappointed and unhappy in love.

Let us examine each of these hypotheses more closely. Tracie's first hypothesis is that there is some dynamic or motive in her psychological makeup that causes her to deliberately select men who are emotionally unavailable. Her statement that "I always choose . . ." acknowledges her belief that her unfortunate fate is somehow under her control and results from some characterological failing of hers. She seems to be blaming herself for the poor love choices that grow out of this unnamed failing. Since she has the conviction that she makes poor choices in men, one of Tracie's conscious goals in coming to therapy has been to "learn to make better choices."

The idea that Tracie makes poor choices reflects her culturally transmitted one-person, isolated-mind view of relationships. She has the experience that relationships haven't worked out, but the meaning she makes of this is that she is at fault because she makes bad choices. She makes a broad leap from experience to explanation. Like Miss K in chapter 2 or Mr. G in chapter 3, Tracie wishes that her therapist would change her by teaching her how to make better choices in men. This reveals Tracie's culturally informed belief that hers is an isolated mind that can be "fixed" by another isolated mind.

In the therapy relationship, Tracie, with her one-person, isolated-mind view of her psychological functioning, finds herself engaged with a therapist who does not share her worldview. Rather, her therapist has a worldview based on an intersubjective systems sensibility. Tracie's therapist, like most psychodynamically oriented therapists, does not believe that his job is to fix her or teach her to choose differently or more wisely. Instead, he believes that change may emerge from their relationship and the new meanings they construct together of her worlds of experience.

If, from the outset, the therapist were to share his sense that he and Tracie are coming to their joint endeavor with different worldviews and treatment aims, Tracie might feel disappointed or, worse, that she has come to the wrong therapist since they have differing visions of how to reach her goal. Instead of provoking an early collision of their differing worlds of experience, Tracie's therapist allowed their philosophical differences to emerge over time and within the dialogue.

When I speak of letting colliding worlds of experience emerge within the therapy process, this might be interpreted as an avoidance of confrontation. It is a familiar critique of self psychology and the intersubjective systems perspectives that we avoid confronting people with their unreasonable thoughts and behaviors in the service of making nice and being liked. As we have discussed previously (Buirski and Haglund 2001), our preference is to focus on the person's worlds of experience and not impose our own structure or agenda on the dialogue—with one exception. We believe that we need to engage the isolated-mind philosophy of the people we work with. Specifically, we address their tendency to blame and pathologize themselves with their culturally embedded isolated-mind perspective on their own thoughts and behaviors because it violates the fundamental assumption of intersubjective systems theory that our subjectivity emerges from relational contexts. The essence of the notion of "confrontation" is that it is something one person, usually the authority or one with power, does to another. When the therapist confronts the other, it is always from a position of greater knowing and privileged authority. Therapists confront people with their transference distortions, their resistances, their acting out behaviors, and so on. On the other hand, collisions, as I am using the term, imply two bodies bumping into each other, neither of which possesses the right of way. While the word "collision" might be construed as aggressive or violent, it is used more to convey a sense that when worlds of experience collide, the impact can be shattering to one's characteristic view of oneself in the world. As my discussion of the dialogue with Tracie unfolds, such collisions will become apparent.

Tracie's worldview, her organization of experience, is that her unhappiness is due to some failing of hers that causes her to be attracted to the wrong men and unexcited by related men. She supposes that she is masochistic. This reflects her isolated-mind perspective that there is something wrong with her, part of which involves some need to bring about her own suffering. From the intersubjective systems perspective, Tracie is indeed bringing her unique organization of experience to any new relationship and this inevitably influences her choices. The treatment question is whether this is a "failing" of hers, as she believes. Are her unsatisfactory choices an outgrowth of some compulsion to repeat, an intrapsychic conflict or of some developmental deficit, or is there some other way to understand this dynamic? From the intersubjective systems perspective, Tracie can be understood as struggling with something crushingly present: her organization of experience that she is defective and flawed and thus rightly to be blamed for the problems in her relationships.

The second implication of this worldview is that it operates unconsciously. Tracie apparently believes that this dynamic operates outside of her conscious awareness and conscious control because she is never aware that it is happening until after the fact. Her statement that "I always choose . . ." carries the tacit acknowledgment that she not only doesn't see it coming, but that her emotional radar may actually be homing in on the "emotionally unavailable men." Accordingly, she implicitly pathologizes herself for her maladaptive, disappointing, and self-defeating choices when it comes to potential partners. If her organizing principles operate unconsciously, then she is helpless to change them by an act of will. She needs the help of an expert to disrupt this dynamic. However, Tracie's intersubjectively oriented therapist, while accepting that her organization of experience may indeed operate outside the horizons of her awareness, does not share her conviction as to the meanings she has made of her experience.

As I have indicated, Tracie believes that there is some fundamental fault in her character that leads her to make unsatisfying choices in men. Tracie pathologizes herself and blames herself for her failings. However, her therapist makes a different set of meanings from her experience. The challenge for this dyad is how to reconcile the differing worldviews, the different meanings that Tracie and her therapist make of her experience. In the process of making sense of Tracie's organization of experience, the therapist and Tracie together constructed a model scene (Lichtenberg, Lachmann, and Fosshage 1992) that built on her descriptions of her childhood and her relationships within her family. Tracie believes that she was viewed as a willful and uncooperative child. The model scene concerned her dress for her confirmation, an important Catholic ceremony held when Tracie was about twelve years old. Tracie, who already had a fashion consciousness at that age, wanted to wear a stylish dress that she had seen in a catalog. Instead, her mother, with her austere and frugal values, thought Tracie should be satisfied with her older sister's conventional dress that could be altered to fit her. In defiance, Tracie used money she had saved from her dog-walking job to order the dress she wanted from the catalog. Although Tracie was permitted to wear the dress she bought, she paid a steep price for her self-assertion. She was berated and ridiculed for being headstrong, rebelliously defiant, and unacceptably deviant from her family's conventional values. Tracie was made to feel ashamed that what she thought was stylish and fashionable, was, in her family's view, ostentatious and flamboyant. This model scene, and numerous other reported incidents of willfulness and oppositional behavior, followed by ridicule and shame, led Tracie to organize her experience around the idea that she was defective and bad. Despite feeling ashamed and unworthy, she continued to resist accommodating to her family's expectations. Why, she wondered, did she persist in these apparently self-defeating behaviors that seemed to only serve to reinforce the conviction that she was a defective and unacceptable child? For Tracie, this was more evidence of her masochism.

Third, Tracie seems to have identified what she considers to be a repetitive pattern when she observes "I always . . ." Thus, Tracie seems to be postulating that she is behaving under the sway of a powerful unconscious dynamic characterized by its repetitive quality: that she is in the grip of some need to repeat that she is doomed to play out over and over. As evidence for this, Tracie reports that she "always chooses unavailable men." However, an interesting ambiguity emerged when Tracie and her therapist examined these failed relationships. All the men were not the same, even though she never married any of them. Some of the relationships ended because Tracie felt unworthy of the men. These men were wealthy and seemed quite accomplished. Whereas Tracie went to her local community college where she studied fashion design, these men had Ivy League educations and Eastern pedigrees. She felt she was wanted only for the sex she could provide and feared that the men would quickly replace her with more attractive, sophisticated women from their social circle. Tracie preemptively ended these relationships before she could be rejected. The men she dated longest tended to be those whom she felt would be proud to be seen with her. While Tracie worked her way up to a job with a major fashion house as a designer, she was drawn to men with blue-collar jobs who made less money than she. Tracie ended some of these relationships when she could not tolerate the men's rejecting behavior, such as flagrantly flirting with or ogling other women. In her experience, even men whom she viewed as beneath her socially could not be depended on to value her. If there was a common theme, it was not that Tracie tended to choose unavailable men, but that because of her low feelings of self-worth, it was hard for her to feel safe, valued, and prized by any man. There were some good men and some not so good men in her dating history, but she could not allow herself to fully trust that any man would want to be with her "'til death did them part."

Tracie's fourth hypothesis about herself was that this repetitive pattern, reflecting some fundamental flaw in her psychological makeup, destined her to be forever disappointed and unhappy in love. She did not feel that her parents valued or admired her and doubted that a man of substance would want her. This conviction about the hopelessness of her romantic future was not entirely consistent with the new relationship that began to develop during the second year of therapy. This new man, an eager young attorney who worked as an in-house counsel for her company, seemed to very much value Tracie. He enjoyed her creativity, energy and intelligence, and sense of humor. He admired her artistic sense and competence at her work and he appreciated her fashion advice on his attire. The theme that was emerging in therapy was whether Tracie could endure the anxiety of being valued by a man she wanted. Did he have other hidden flaws besides the poor judgment to find her worthy? How long would it be before he tired of her and how much risk of inevitable hurt could she tolerate?

One might hear an Oedipal theme here: that Tracie might break up with men over her guilt about their unconscious resemblance to her rejecting father. This would be consistent with a classical view of intrapsychic conflict between forbidden longings and guilt. However, the pain of guilt over unacceptable longings is quite a different formulation from shame over feeling unworthy and the anticipation of the hurt of rejection. It might actually have been easier for Tracie to accept such an Oedipal interpretation because it fit with her isolated-mind view of herself as flawed and bad. Now, we often believe as therapists, that the acceptance of an interpretation, and perhaps the generation of confirming associations, is the measure of a correct interpretation. Accepting it might even reflect some wish to please her analyst. From the intersubjective systems perspective, however, the acceptance of such an Oedipal interpretation might merely reflect a conjunction between Tracie's organization of experience and her therapist's theory-driven understanding; they both would share the conviction that her unconscious mind is filled with unacceptable contents.

Tracie's developmental experience of having been treated as though she was unacceptably rebellious, willful, defective, and shamefully flawed had become the foundation for her organization of experience. Her therapist, by contrast, had a different view of her worlds of experience that collided with Tracie's. Her therapist viewed Tracie's rebellion as a measure of her striving for health. He articulated an alternative vision, not of a defective and flawed young girl, but of a fighter whose willful self-assertion was her saving grace. What her family defined as her defects, her therapist saw as her strength. From his perspective, rather than shame, Tracie might take pride in her refusal to surrender her autonomous self-organization, in the willful defense of her threatened sense of personal agency. He saw Tracie, not as oppositional, defiant, and stubborn, but as having saved her own emotional life through her refusal to surrender her self-hood.

As Tracie's story began to unfold, her therapist articulated a different way of making sense of her experience. Together they reconstructed her organization of experience, and the therapist articulated an alternate set of meanings that could be made of her childhood: that she was different, not flawed; that she was artistic, not defiant; that she was strong, not rebellious; that she did not purposely seek out unavailable men, but had difficulty trusting that someone would truly value her. Regarding men, Tracie was sexually attracted to men whom she felt were "dating up." She only felt safe when she thought that the man was thrilled to be with a woman like her. However, when deep connections to a man began to form, Tracie felt anxious, suddenly unaroused, and began the withdrawal process. The issue became reformulated in terms of whether Tracie could maintain her attraction in the face of her expectation of inevitable rejection and disappointment.

Tracie and her therapist first collided when, rather than accept that she was solely to blame for her fiancé's gambling and stealing, her therapist described the power of addiction and the futility of her assuming the blame for her fiancé's actions and of trying to change him by becoming a better person. Tracie, her therapist believed, didn't drive the fiancé to gamble, but perhaps was enabling him by assuming the blame was hers alone. This began the process of disconfirming her four hypotheses and depathologizing her convictions about the nature of her defectiveness. This provoked a dramatic collision of worldviews where, for example, Tracie scowled at her therapist and said, "You are not supposed to be supporting me and making me feel good. You are supposed to be pointing out my flaws and helping me change them!" On other occasions, Tracie suggested that the therapist meet with the fiancé so that the therapist could hear the truth about her, since he had apparently been fooled by her presentation. After several months, Tracie ended the relationship with her fiancé. As a measure of her strengthening self-organization, Tracie came to appreciate that breaking the engagement was not a repetition of the same old pattern, but was a measure of her enhanced sense of self-worth.

At another point, her therapist depathologized Tracie's view that she was fooling her boss at work since he failed to see the inadequacy of her designs. Her therapist articulated that, "It is hard to conceive that others could value you when you have grown up feeling so devalued in your family. You have concluded from your experience that you are defective and worthless. Anyone who sees you differently is not to be trusted." To this, Tracie said snidely, "You only say nice things about me because I pay you!" And her therapist replied, "When your view of you and my view of you differ, it must be that I am lying or blowing smoke; that I, too, am not to be trusted." Later on her therapist asked, "How do we reconcile our two different views of you?"

Tracie's complex four-part theory of how her mind operates regarding her relational functioning will find some conjunction with certain psychoanalytic theories. It seems plausible that both contemporary Freudian and modern relational theories would have no difficulty accepting the four critical factors of her theory: the causative motive, its unconscious operation, its repetitive quality, and the fundamental character flaw that underlies the first three factors and dooms her to unhappiness. The fact that there are points of conjunction between Tracie's theories of mind and the theories of many therapists makes it likely that both will view the validity of Tracie's theory of mind as self-evident. When the therapist not only understands but agrees with the person's way of viewing herself and her predicament, one might suspect that this would be a clear example of conjunction or empathic attunement in action. Clearly, though, there is an important difference between understanding the meanings one has made from one's experience and validating the self-blaming and pathologizing that these meanings carry with them.

Tracie came to her session some time later, berating herself for having gotten drunk the night before with friends. She rarely drinks excessively and feels ashamed of herself for engaging in behavior she views as self-destructive. She was up late, overslept, and came late for her session with a hangover. She was remorseful and self-critical. In her session, the therapist commented that she was very harsh with herself. Tracie has not been an alcohol abuser, has a very good work ethic, and has become very successful. She was dismissive of the therapist's depathologizing comments and told him he should not be supportive of her bad behavior. Rather, he should be critical of her and disappointed in her. The therapist again articulated Tracie's organization of experience— that she believes she is defective and flawed and unworthy of support. He again pointed out that her experience is organized around the notion that she is inferior and unworthy and that she dismisses as mistaken, foolish, or gullible anyone, including the therapist, who does not confirm or share that view. The next session Tracie came in and said, "I felt so relieved, like a weight had been lifted off me after last session."

These are but a few of the multitude of examples from this particular treatment where the meanings derived from the experience of the two participants collided. When worlds of experience collide, it is not a matter of one person being right and the other being wrong, but of there being different ways of viewing the world, different meanings that can be made of experience. Making sense of this discrepancy can be challenging. It was disorganizing for Tracie to have thrown into doubt her way of making sense of the world, and this could only be done over a long period of time and in the context of a secure selfobject relationship. Reconciling colliding worldviews occurs as an unfolding process, not by one person convincing the other of the truth of his or her vision. The organization of experience that a person brings to treatment has been formed within a relational developmental context of experience with caregivers and other influential people. The formation of new ways of organizing one's experience can only take place in a new relational engagement that doesn't make sense when viewed through the old lens.

How, for example, is Tracie to understand that another person, her therapist, sees her as strong, worthy, and likable? At first, Tracie dealt with these discrepant versions of herself by complaining that the therapist did not understand her. However, over time, Tracie had to admit that her therapist did understand much of her experience, but his vision made no sense to her. Later, she dismissed her therapist as a sycophant (or psychophant as she joked) who just tried to butter her up because she paid him. But her joke betrayed that she really was having difficulty believing this.

Over time, Tracie had to acknowledge that she just felt so much better about herself. She was advancing in her work, felt increasing self-confidence, and her boss began talking about giving Tracie her own clothing line. She may have thought that he, too, was crazy, but the sales numbers where hard to deny. In another challenging development, Tracie's new boyfriend was able to accept that she did not feel ready to make a commitment. Tracie needed more time and he was prepared to wait for her, even though this meant that she would also date other men. He communicated that he loved her and that he could be patient while Tracie sorted out her feelings. It was difficult for Tracie to make sense of her boyfriend's commitment, especially since sex had been put on hold. Since Tracie did not perceive him to be "dating up," what did he see in her? What was she good for?

Colliding worlds of experience between members of the therapy dyad provides the opportunity for new ways of organizing experience to be constructed. Tracie could begin to question her organization of experience that she was flawed and defective when faced with a disconfirming view of her that was offered by her therapist. She must either maintain her organization of experience by dismissing him or she must begin to open her view of herself to further examination and revision. However, what is most significant is not that Tracie came to assimilate the alternative meanings that she and her therapist made of her formative and current experience, but that her view of herself in the world began to change. She came to see herself as worthy, desirable, and substantial. She felt good about herself, confident in her abilities and trusting of her own judgment. And the lawyer proved not to be another emotionally unavailable man, but a man with whom she could work through her fear of rejection.

After this chapter was written, it was shared with Tracie. She had some powerful reactions. She cried when she read it because she felt validated and understood. Someone else was bearing witness to her struggles and appreciating what she had been through. On the other hand, the thought occurred to her that maybe the therapist had written this as a part of her treatment. She laughingly recognized this thought as the familiar use of doubt to minimize the impact of the colliding of their two views of her experience. But most revealingly, Tracie said that the written discussion had struck a chord with a little voice within her that protested the invalidation of her experience that she felt subjected to during her childhood. For Tracie and for many others in similar situations, the collision of worlds of experience carries the potential to shatter archaic organizations of experience and transform into new ones because, on some deep level, the person has always known, but felt pressure to disavow, this alternative vision of her- or himself in the world.

Chapter Five

An Intersubjective Systems Perspective on Multicultural Treatment

Coauthored with Michelle Doft, PsyD

The practice of psychotherapy in the last decade has been especially concerned with evidence-based or empirically supported treatment modalities (Crits-Christoph et al. 1995). However, this focus on evidence-based treatments has tended to neglect the cultural context within which treatments occur. In our increasingly pluralistic society, it would be a mistake to assume that treatments validated on one cultural population are generalizable to all.

One contemporary criticism of psychology and psychoanalysis has been that the fields lack an appreciation of the cultural contexts of people's lives, including the discriminatory practices directed toward minority groups (Sue and Sue 1999). As Sue and Sue (1999) noted, "The need for our profession and psychologists to address issues of race, culture, and ethnicity has never been more urgent" (p. 3). Despite what appears to be widespread agreement that there is a critical need to prepare mental health professionals to provide sensitive and effective services to cultural minorities, there continues to be "inappropriate service delivery, consumer dissatisfaction, and reluctance toward future psychological service utilization" (Kazarian and Evans 1998, p. 13). Given the cultural transformation that has been occurring, D'Andrea (2003) has observed that the failure to adapt therapeutic practice to cultural contexts will result in an undermining of the credibility and viability of our nation's mental healthcare system.

For psychoanalysis, the traditional approach has been criticized for being not only ineffective with minorities, but also inherently oppressive (Toukmanian and Brouwers 1998). There has been a striking lack of research as to how psychoanalytic theory and technique might be applied with multicultural populations (Mishne 2002). For the most part, the psychoanalytic literature has not addressed concerns related to the treatment needs of ethnic and racial minorities. However, contemporary psychoanalytic approaches, with their emphasis on relational and contextual influences, seem to offer culturally sensitive approaches to multicultural populations in need of service.

Ironically, one of the major cultural forces that has led to the development of the relational movement in contemporary psychoanalysis has been the work of the Stone Center (Jordan 1997) and the influence of the women's movement. Leary (2002) notes that "Feminist critiques have powerfully illustrated the way in which such (psychoanalytic) presumptions reinforced hierarchies of power that marginalized women's experience in the consulting room and society at large" (p. 314). The Stone Center theorists (Jordan 1997) have instigated a necessary paradigm shift for Western psychology toward relationship and intersubjective experience and away from separateness of self. This expansion of theory fits the diversity of all human experience, as opposed to focusing primarily on the experience of the privileged.

This chapter, then, will examine the theoretical and clinical constraints that traditional psychoanalytically oriented psychotherapies bring to multicultural treatment. We will then contrast these with a more relational and intersubjective psychoanalytic perspective that, we believe, better lends itself to working with culturally diverse populations. In particular, we will discuss how practicing intersubjectively can minimize some of the pitfalls of traditional theoretical approaches by sensitively and effectively engaging both members of the therapy dyad who themselves may come from different ethnic and racial backgrounds.

MULTICULTURALISM AND PSYCHOTHERAPY

In August 2002, the American Psychological Association (APA) issued a document entitled *Guidelines on Multicultural Education, Training, Research, Practice, and Organizational Change for Psychologists* in an effort to address the need for greater multicultural sensitivity. The racial, ethnic, and religious differences that are present in the members of the therapy dyad are important and unavoidable contextual components that impact the relationship and engagement of the participants.

The relevance of context is a key point that is reiterated in the APA guidelines (2002). There are a variety of contextual variables that affect participants in the therapy dyad, including generational history, citizenship, language, level of education, socioeconomic status, work history, history of acculturation and accompanying stresses, and experiences of racism and oppression. Clearly, all people exist in social, political, historic, and economic contexts; the influence of such contexts on emotional development and social adjustment cannot be underestimated or ignored.

Stuart (2004) defines multicultural competence as "the ability to understand and constructively relate to the uniqueness of each client in light of the diverse cultures that influence each person's perspectives" (p. 3). However, for most practitioners, multicultural competence is constrained by our theory of mental functioning. One limitation of the multicultural applicability of many psychoanalytic constructs and theories arises from the fact that these notions were developed within a Western worldview.

A worldview refers to the way that individuals experience the world and their relationships within it. Worldviews can be understood as overarching frameworks that consist of "different beliefs, presuppositions, and assumptions that influence and guide the way in which we perceive, evaluate and interpret events in everyday life situations" (Toukmanian and Brouwers 1998, p. 117). Worldviews develop from experience and are influenced by factors that are specific to each individual. Insofar as psychoanalytically oriented psychotherapy is a phenomenon of Western culture, it is reflective of a worldview rooted in Western values and philosophical/ideological assumptions.

Mio and Iwamasa (2003) call our attention to the fact that our Western models of treatment could be experienced by people of different cultural backgrounds as inherently oppressive; that embedded in our theories are monocultural and ethnocentric views of mental health that might perpetuate oppression. Theories that are decidedly Anglo-Saxon in their conceptions of human nature may be philosophically and culturally limited; as such, they may be incompatible with multiculturally sensitive treatment (Gilbert and Evans 2000).

The medical model, for example, which is reflective of a Western worldview, is a dominant framework used by mental health professionals to understand and treat "psychiatric" problems. By focusing on objectivist and authority-based views of treatment, this framework fosters a hierarchical therapist–patient relationship with an emphasis on professional expertise and knowledge and patient dependency. From this perspective, the professional knows and "interprets" meaning for the patient. This hierarchical relationship, with its implicit power imbalance, may be experienced by minority groups as oppressive. The medical model can lead to unintentional racism, as therapists operating within it tend to reduce social problems to intrapsychic processes and to overpathologize individuals (Gilbert and Evans 2000). Alienation and mistrust also may play key roles in the difficulty that occurs in cross-cultural therapy dyads. It is not uncommon for people of color to feel lonely and estranged, and to enter the therapeutic relationship assuming that they will be pushed away or misunderstood, as they so often have been in society (Mishne 2002, p. 69).

MULTICULTURAL LIMITATIONS
OF PSYCHOANALYTIC THEORIES

In this section, we will expand on the idea that traditional psychoanalytic theory, with its one-person, authority-based, objectivist stance, is at variance with contemporary multicultural perspectives. While there has been a shift in the psychoanalytic field toward more relational work, contemporary Freudian theory is still largely impacted by a philosophy that does not lend itself to working with multicultural populations. Such traditions extend far back in psychoanalytic history influencing and "obscuring the intersubjective nature of the analytic process" (Yi 1998, p. 249) so that a critique of multicultural insensitivity seems warranted.

Altman (1995) pointed out that psychoanalytic treatment has "created an environment for itself that is the functional equivalent of a homogenous American suburban environment with respect to culture, class, and race" (p. xvii). Jackson (2001) notes that "Communities of color have long been suspicious of psychoanalytic models because of their traditional focus on the individual, as well as their failure to acknowledge racist and sexist assumptions underlying the theory of personality development" (p. 1). Leary (1995), in a critique of traditional psychoanalytic treatment with racial and ethnic minorities, cites one of the reasons for a lack of focus on racial and ethnic issues as being related to these topics remaining taboo both in society and in clinical practice. As Leary (1995) has observed, "Discussion about race is either avoided altogether or quickly dispensed with after only superficial consideration and with a sigh of relief" (p. 128).

A major critique of psychoanalytic approaches is that they maintain a basic premise that problems in living originate within the isolated mind of the individual (Stolorow and Atwood 1992). From this perspective, which regards the person's internal mental processes as the locus of psychopathology, the responsibility for change rests primarily with the individual. This premise is based on Cartesian philosophy that posits the mind as an objective thing that looks out on the world, from which it is separate. The assumptions of traditional psychoanalytic theory cannot be separated from the Cartesian doctrine of the isolated mind (Orange, Atwood, and Stolorow 1997). Thus, the very foundation of traditional psychoanalysis minimizes the contexts that shape people in the world. For example, in traditional Freudian theory, by virtue of our common biology, all people are thought to struggle with conflicts over their shared antisocial drives. Therefore, all people can be treated with the same therapeutic approach of making the unconscious conscious and replacing id with ego.

While this uniform approach seems more plausible in the area of medicine, it often fails there, too. For example, since tuberculosis is caused by a bacteria, the *Mycobacterium tuberculosis*, then any human being, regardless of culture, will be susceptible to contracting the disease if exposed. However, as Farmer (2003) has documented in his extraordinary book, *Pathologies of Power*, the rates of tuberculosis contraction are very much dependent on sociocultural conditions, such as poverty, that influence hygiene and nutrition. Since psychopathology has been seen as deriving from universal human characteristics, there has been little room for an investigation of how cultural context will shape treatment. Oppression, racism, poverty, and other culturally relevant factors may contribute to personality development as well as to diagnosis. Many critics believe that traditional psychoanalytic theory has not recognized the "enormous weight of culture in the application of orthodox, rigid concepts to the interactive reality of patient and therapist" (Alarcon, Foulks, and Vakkur 1998, p. 210).

The potential neglect of situational or contextual factors forms the basis of another major criticism of psychoanalytic theory (Toukmanian and Brouwers 1998). According to critics, the traditional psychoanalytic assumption that the innate potential of an individual will thrive when matched with good enough care giving and an average expectable environment is not sufficient, and is "hopelessly passive in the face of problematic social and political structures" (Samuels 1993, p. 583). According to Mishne (2002), contextual factors typically neglected by psychoanalysis include but are not limited to environmental factors, life circumstances, institutional racism, and discrimination. When therapists operating within the psychoanalytic model do recognize such factors, many critics believe that these factors are of secondary importance in case conceptualization and treatment planning. However, as the APA (2002) recently pointed out, contexts need to be recognized as both members of the therapy dyad are influenced by historical, ecological, economic, and sociopolitical contexts.

The familiar psychoanalytic constructs of transference and countertransference, as they are used in psychoanalytic literature, put the focus on what goes on within the isolated minds of the participants and overlook the coconstructed nature of the intersubjective field. Despite growing agreement that therapists cannot be neutral, such a stance is often held as "a revered, albeit unattainable ideal" (Orange, Atwood, and Stolorow 1997, p. 36). According to Orange, Atwood, and Stolorow (1997), therapists may be more likely to attempt neutrality when transferential expressions "threaten essential features of their sense of self" (p. 36). When cultural differences evoke anxiety within therapists, they may defend against their disruptive feelings by claiming neutrality or colorblindness. This maneuver ignores the person of the therapist, who undoubtedly holds preconceptions that enter the room. When these preconceptions are left unexamined, they "can and do create barriers of inordinate proportions" (Mishne 2002, p. 24).

Constructs, like transference and countertransference, viewed as arising within the isolated minds of the participants, neglect what is seen as vital in multiculturally sensitive therapy; that is, the context within which treatment occurs. The context of the therapy room clearly includes cultural features of the therapist that cannot be neutral (Yi 1998). On the other hand, to be a relational psychoanalyst means to recognize the co-construction of experience for both participants (Aron 1996). A therapeutic stance that deemphasizes the therapist's impact on the other's experience does not leave room to explore the manner in which the therapist's subjectivity—and thus, the therapist's culture—enters the room. From a multicultural perspective in particular, an awareness of mutual influence, co-construction of experience, and the contextual foundations of intersubjective systems can promote mutual understanding and a collaborative working relationship.

Race-based transference has been explained within the psychoanalytic literature "as a manifestation of the patient's intrapsychic instinctual conflicts" or as "a defensively motivated projection of the undesirable aspects of the self onto the race of the therapist" (Yi 1998, p. 246). Yi described this view of transference as adverse, because the therapist is "conveniently left out from the question as to how she or he might contribute to the development of race-based transference" (p. 248).

Notions of countertransference include both the therapist's reactions to the other's transference as well as the transferential meaning the other has for the therapist (Mishne 2002). However, such formulations both derive from isolated-mind perspectives and do not engage the contextual influences on the intersubjective field. The impact of such isolated-mind perspectives on transference and countertransference serves to narrow the focus of the therapist, not only neglecting the fact that both participants "integrate not only the content of the interaction, but also information about the target person, including personality traits, physical appearance, age, sex, ascribed race, ability/disability, among other characteristics" (APA 2002, p. 19). Alternatively, contemporary relational psychoanalytic approaches, because of their emphasis on co-construction, mutual regulation, and contextual influences, are very viable, culturally sensitive approaches to the therapeutic engagement of people from diverse backgrounds.

Both participants in a treatment inevitably hold prereflective or unconscious biases and attitudes that guide their engagement with each other. By acknowledging and becoming more aware of our own potentially culturally limiting beliefs, psychotherapists can avoid operating in a colorblind manner, ignoring racial and ethnic differences that are vital to self-organization. The APA guidelines caution against an emphasis on universal aspects of human behavior (and corresponding deemphasis of cultural differences) that fits with the "melting pot" metaphor that has only served to maintain the status quo.

INTERSUBJECTIVE SYSTEMS THEORY
AS A CULTURALLY SENSITIVE TREATMENT

The diversity of Western culture has provided the psychoanalytic field with an opportunity to engage in productive introspection through which it may examine its limitations and make necessary changes (Bucci 2002). Leary (1995) points out that "the psychoanalytic situation may offer a unique opportunity for elaborating the meaning of race and ethnicity to the extent that the analytic clinician can focus on the amalgams of fantasy and reality to which talk about race is heir and discover the idiosyncratic purposes to which it has been put" (p. 133). It is clear that a far-reaching multicultural sensitivity calls for a contextualization of all aspects of human life. As Perlmutter (1996) observed, "cultural responsiveness requires an appreciation of the importance of intersubjective experiences, because culture is so intrinsic to subjective experiences" (p. 390).

Intersubjective systems theory is centrally concerned with the impact of contextual and systemic factors on the subjective worlds of experience of individuals (Buirski and Haglund 2001). Rejecting the traditional psychoanalytic stance that the therapist can have objective knowledge of the other person, intersubjective systems theory replaces this belief with a view that recognizes that both participants have unique subjectively experienced realities, "one not any more objective or valid than the other" (Yi 1998, p. 251). From the intersubjective systems perspective, therapeutic neutrality is an impossibility, as the worlds of experience of both participants shape and influence the intersubjective field. In its contention that subjective emotional experience is regulated from birth onward within ongoing relational systems, intersubjective systems theory offers an alternative to the classical notions of drives that originate within the isolated mind (Stolorow, Atwood, and Orange 2002). The intersubjective systems sensibility, with its central focus on the contextual construction of experience, makes it a viable, flexible, and multiculturally compatible perspective for clinical work with cultural minorities.

THE CONCEPTUALIZATION
OF A MULTICULTURAL CONTEXT

Since worlds of experience for both participants in the therapy dyad are subjectively organized, neither will see the world exactly as the other participant does (Buirski and Haglund 2001). This is especially pertinent in therapy dyads where both parties come from different cultural, racial, ethnic, or religious backgrounds. From an intersubjective systems perspective, understanding the subjective organization of the world of experience of another necessarily includes the various contextual factors that have contributed to its unique development. Orange, Atwood, and Stolorow (1997) emphasize the contextual nature of intersubjectivity, as it "includes the interacting subjective worlds and the organizing activities of both patient and analyst, including the analyst's theories and the cultural worlds of both participants" (p. 77). While intersubjective systems theory appreciates that the principles that organize experience take form in the early environment, we recognize that cultural contexts are an inseparable component of any environment and therefore also play an important part in the organization of the individual's experience. Culture is imbedded in experience and cannot be separated from it. Culture is one of many interactive contextual factors that influences how all unique individuals come to experience themselves in the world and make sense of that experience. All individuals create subjective meaning within the parameters of their particular culture and life experience.

Culture plays a particularly significant role in the construction of emotion, as children learn how and where to express emotions based on cultural guidelines. Our affects can be seen as culturally rooted, in that culture is experienced daily as a system that is embedded in life through social relations, activities, and institutions. Experiences related to culture may contribute to the formation of a template, that we then use to organize our experiences, thoughts, feelings, and behaviors. The creation of meaning is at once cultural, personal, and idiosyncratic. Humans define their subjective reality, often unconsciously, through the organization of meaning that develops within a particular cultural milieu.

Anthropologists use a cultural constructivist view of human emotion. Within this perspective, human emotions depend on cultural concepts; thus, the meaning of events and norms for emotional responses are not uniform across cultures. Cultural constructivists argue that it is necessary to understand the possible cultural schemas that have an impact on emotions (Castillo 1997). The impact of race and ethnicity on the development of subjectivity is profound (Yi 1998). Identity conflicts occur when individuals perceive and simultaneously reject attributes of themselves. Awareness of oneself as a person of color, for instance, may be rejected in favor of the white models that are pervasive in our society. It is difficult for people to value themselves when who they are is not valued by the larger social context. Identity conflict seems inevitable when one experiences being different as being inferior. The integration and regulation of affective experience are integral to the formation of identity. The larger social environment, structured by the majority culture, has a huge impact on how minorities develop a cohesive and positive self-organization.

When selfobject functions are not provided on a consistent basis in the cultural milieu, a person may come to believe that he or she is not "good enough." A child may develop a similar belief if his or her early care-giving environment fails to provide necessary affectively attuned experiences. In a misattuned care-giving environment, children may organize their experiences by believing that they are "wrong" or "bad," rather than by attaching such labels to the caregiver who has failed to provide protection. This may also happen when members of a minority group have repeated interpersonal experiences related to their race and then begin to organize these experiences and to build a template. When the social climate is not good enough, for instance, a Hispanic woman may come to see herself as "bad" and the majority culture as "good."

In her therapy practice, White (2002) observed that many of the people of color that she worked with had come to see *themselves*, rather than their social context, as bad. White desired to teach them that "racism is ugly, not you; racism is evil, not you; racism is baleful, not you; racism is malignant and malevolent, not you" (p. 409). In discussing her experience as an African American therapist working with African American people, White stated, "many patients come into psychoanalysis attributing being hated or hating to something akin to original sin, or genetic flaw, feeling somewhat like Rosemary's baby—evil and satanic" (p. 406). According to White, being hated can become "a self-definition, safety operation, and defense" (p. 406). She went on to describe a "survival shell" that she has witnessed with African Americans, which speaks to the risk that is involved in living in the context of hatred. Concerning one black person she worked with, White observed, "in her bones she is convinced that she is doomed to hatefulness by reason of her genetic makeup; in my bones, I hope she is wrong" (p. 407).

From the intersubjective systems perspective, the core of psychopathology concerns an individual's difficulty with the integration and modulation of affect (Buirski and Haglund 2001). While a person of color may have received good enough parenting—which normally leads to the ability to articulate, regulate, and integrate affect—trauma in the form of racism and oppression can compromise his or her development in this regard. Gump (2000) describes slavery as "the ultimate mortification, for there is no abasement as profound as what destroys subjectivity, which says through work or action, 'what you need, what you desire, and what you feel are of complete and utter insignificance'" (p. 625). While mass genocide and slavery can be seen as obvious traumatic events for cultures, the less obvious and more modern forms of oppression are often given less attention. Oppression, as experienced on a regular basis by some individuals, can be experienced as traumatic. Leary (2002) describes such daily intrusions as micro-traumas that over time can "erode the self" (p. 641). And, while tragedies like slavery or the Holo-caust happened generations ago, the intergenerational transmission of trauma is well documented (Danieli 1985).

The notion of the intergenerational transmission of trauma alludes to the close relationship between subjectivity and culture. A Jewish individual in the present time, for instance, may develop a subjectivity that is shaped by knowledge of the Holocaust. A history in which it was necessary to hide Jewish identity to survive has resulted in some Jews developing their organ-ization of experience around the principle that they will only be accepted by others and able to connect with them if they mask their Jewish heritage. As a result, affectivity may be disavowed to maintain perceived—and, perhaps, actual—psychological and physical safety. This may also be true of Native Americans, whose ancestors were forced to attend boarding schools and to give up their Indian clothing and jewelry to survive in a hostile environment. The enormous empathic failures experienced by slaves and the pain associ-ated with destruction of subjectivity "reverberates in the parenting practices of too many African American families" (Gump 2000, p. 627). There is a psychological legacy that is inevitable in many descendants and this fear—as an intergenerational trauma—may still be alive and may be dealt with by shutting off certain emotions.

When central affect states evoke massive misattunement from environ-mental surroundings, they may be defensively walled off or disavowed. Indi-viduals seeking to avoid retraumatization may use this disavowal of affect states as a means of self-protection. When attuned responsiveness is not pro-vided, central affect states cannot be integrated, as they fail to evoke such responses. These affect states become a source of conflict because they are experienced as a threat to the person's invariant organization of experience and to the maintenance of needed ties to objects.

Effective therapy promotes the identification and articulation of central affects that promote their integration and regulation. Selfobject experience promotes the integration of affect, promoting self-cohesion and the building of positive self-esteem. Howard (1991) stated that "empathic experiencing is perhaps the psychotherapist's greatest aid in escaping our inevitable lim-itations in understanding people from different culture, races, belief sys-tems, sexes, places and time" (p. 196). Speaking of an entire society gripped by racial hatred and persecution, Pumla Gobodo-Madikizela (2003), a clin-ical psychologist and a member of the South African Truth and Reconcilia-tion Commission, described empathy as "a profound gift in this brutal world we have created for one another as people of different races, creeds, and political persuasions" (p. 139). White (2002) expressed the hope that, through treatment, "new propositions can be developed from new and different experiences through the emotional lessons of our analytic relationship" (p. 409).

From the intersubjective systems perspective, the therapeutic relationship is the field within which thwarted developmental longings can be remobilized and fulfilled. In social contexts where suspicion and mistrust between the cultures have been pervasive, the development of trust and acceptance in a cross-racial or cross-cultural therapeutic dyad can be challenging. We will now describe one such mixed therapeutic dyad and the challenges that both parties faced in constructing their relationship. Since we believe that culture, race, and ethnicity have unique personal meanings for each individual, some of which are no doubt shared by other members of the group, we need to be careful to avoid stereotyped generalizations from the particular individual, to the larger cultural group to which she belongs. This is a dyad specific discussion, within which issues of cross-cultural difference play a role. In the therapy relationship discussed below, Michelle Doft, PsyD, was the therapist.

CASE STUDY: ANNA

Anna's case is presented as an example of how cultural context has influenced the organization of experience of one Latina female. This discussion will also highlight the intersubjective field and some of the challenges that arose for this therapy dyad, who come from different racial contexts. Anna was a twenty-seven-year-old female who pursued therapy for two years. When she entered therapy at an adult outpatient clinic, Anna complained of low self-esteem and difficulty asserting herself and reported that she was having trouble in her marital relationship. Anna was married to a white male, whom she felt she could not please. It was at his insistence that she initially entered treatment, as he had convinced her that she was "the problem." Anna had organized her experience in such a way that she had come to feel invisible, unimportant, defective, and bad.

During treatment, Anna always arrived early for sessions and was always dressed neatly and professionally. This, we learned, was an adaptive accommodation that furthered her need to find emotional safety by fitting in to the white world in which she lived and worked. Early in therapy, she came to sessions and presented material that she had prepared for discussion. She often smiled and rarely expressed negative emotions, even when talking about events that seemed uncomfortable or troubling. It was apparent that Anna had a difficult time expressing her emotions and clearly did not believe that her feelings were valid. Anna often had a headache or described feeling "tired," but she did not seem to have the vocabulary for articulating affective states.

English was Anna's first language and, while she had an extensive vocabulary, it was clear that she lacked the words to describe her feelings. Anna canceled sessions a few times, leaving lengthy messages explaining that she had an emergency at work that required her to stay late. Over time, it emerged that Anna felt she was unwelcome in the white world. She believed she was a burden to her therapist, whom she sought to placate. She imagined that her therapist was bored and would prefer her not to show up. Also, she felt powerless and struggled with setting limits with her boss. Thus, she often felt pressured to accommodate to her boss's demand that she work long hours and complete extra projects.

Together, Anna and her therapist learned that her organization of experience was partially based on conclusions drawn from early childhood relationships. She believed that her mother and father had always favored her brother, who was culturally valued as a male, while they viewed her as an incompetent female. Even though she worked hard as a child to gain recognition from her family, she never felt "seen." Anna learned that if she kept quiet and did everything "perfectly," she could avoid experiencing feelings of anger and pain. Since her affects were systematically invalidated, she concluded that these "bad" feelings were unacceptable; they were discouraged and only seemed to cause trouble in her relationships with others. Thus, she disavowed these feelings. This process was protective and helped Anna to avoid the verbal berating that was inevitable with "even the slightest complaint of discomfort." When Anna became the first member of her family to attend college, she waited for her family to acknowledge and enjoy her success. Instead, they condemned her for not having prospects for marriage.

As Anna began to express her sadness and disappointment about these experiences of failed attunement, she also began to recognize parallel experiences in her current relationship with her new husband. She was extremely conflicted about her role in the relationship, given her previous experience with the cultural expectations of her family. Anna began to identify feeling angry that she was expected to take care of the marital household with no help from her husband. Another indication of her second-class status was that they never watched what she wanted on TV. The articulation of this anger also evoked shame because Anna felt under the pressure of cultural expectations that she take care of her husband and "never complain."

It became clear that Anna's subjective experience was not only formed in her early relational experiences with her family, but were also shaped in relation to the larger social climate that impacted the family. At a very young age, Anna noticed that she and her family received discriminatory treatment, and she connected this with the color of their skin. At restaurants, they often waited longer than others to be seated or were not seated at all. Throughout school, Anna always felt as if she were "on the outside looking in" and came to understand this as being related to her skin color. Anna remembers "trying everything to fit in," but the color of her skin, which she could not change, was the only thing that kept her from getting the attention she craved. Anna came to see the color of her skin and her heritage as sources of shame. She longed to shed her color and all of the disadvantages and shame that she felt came with it. At work it was no different—Anna had many experiences of feeling ignored and overlooked by others and she often saw Caucasian coworkers promoted ahead of her. Anna always felt that she was the one getting the "short end of the stick" and was left feeling that it was because there was something wrong with her.

When Anna met her husband, she initially felt that he had things to offer that she had never experienced before. He was white, and she felt better about herself when she was with him, as if doors were opened that had previously been shut. In therapy, Anna explored her experience with him, and both participants began to understand how different, yet similar, he was to her family caregivers. Anna initially began to express "annoyance" and later anger that she had spent much of her money on buying a big-screen TV for their house to make her husband happy, despite her not getting to watch what she wanted to see. She felt that his wishes were more important than hers, and he reinforced this message on a daily basis. Anna described feeling "oppressed" in the relationship and began to feel angry that she was unable to discover herself and felt "like a slave." When Anna began to express her feeling to her husband in situations where she felt oppressed because of her color, her husband yelled at her for "taking things too seriously." Again, Anna felt misunderstood, invalidated, and unimportant.

In the past, the reactions to Anna's expression of anger made her feel "crazy" or "too sensitive," especially where racial issues were concerned. She believed that expression of such feelings would only distance her from her goals of fitting in and pleasing people. Anna worried that her anger would destroy her relationships with her husband and her boss and did not want to risk such losses. Once, when Anna was traveling in the Deep South on business, a clerk closed the line in a store just as she approached, and she felt crushed. In therapy, she wondered, "Was I hated for my brown skin, or was I simply not noticed at all?" Anna's experience was organized, not only around her feeling of being invisible and worthless in her family, but also by similar feelings in her dealings with the white culture at large. Anna's therapist began to wonder what it was like for Anna to work with her, a white therapist. It seemed inevitable, given Anna's experiences in the white culture, that her therapist's skin color would impact her and influence what she imagined her therapist thought of her.

On one occasion, Anna was late for therapy due to rush hour traffic and she arrived at the clinic in a panic. She appeared frazzled and was crying. She said over and over how sorry she was and she imagined her therapist would be angry with her. Anna was ashamed and feared that she had "really messed up." When asked if there was an aspect of her therapist that played into this worry, Anna hesitantly revealed that her white skin color had a great deal of influence on her feeling. She assumed that she would only be accepted by her therapist if she acted "perfect," which meant always arriving early, appearing professional, and having "nothing out of place." Anna's experience with white people in authority was that she was overlooked if she did not appear this way, and these experiences had left her feeling, once again, invisible and worthless.

Anna's familial situation in many ways paralleled the way that she felt in society at large, as if she could never be good enough. It was often difficult to determine whether Anna's feelings and behaviors were related to being female in her family, to being Hispanic in the white culture at large, or to her relationship with her therapist and what she represented to her. Would her therapist view her as her mother did, or was her therapist an agent of the white culture, or both? It was a measure of Anna's growing trust in her therapist's attunement that she was able to disclose her fear and shame in therapy. Though her feelings were initially quite intense, disorganizing, and painful for her, her courage furthered their mutual understanding.

As therapy progressed and the relationship strengthened, Anna began to feel accepted, affirmed, and safe. She became more aware and more articulate about her varied affects. The identification and articulation of previously unformulated and disavowed affects, in a safe environment with a white person, enabled Anna to begin to construct new ways of organizing her experience. As she formed new organizing principles, her behavior began to change. In therapy, Anna's organization of experience began to shift, as revealed by articulations like, "It really isn't fair. I never thought before that I had the right to ask for anything. I was always afraid. It is not fair for me to have been belittled, and I think I deserve better." Anna expressed these feelings following an incident in which her boss treated her poorly after she requested the day off for her birthday. Such an articulation stood in stark contrast to earlier expressions of self-hatred and worthlessness. A year earlier, her primary reaction would have been deep fear and great shame about communicating a need or want.

These and other expressions of formerly disavowed affects indicated that Anna was forming new organizations of experience, involving her relation to her own and the majority culture. By the end of the therapy, it was clear that these previously disorganizing affects were becoming more integrated within her self-organization. It seemed that the safe and affirming context of the therapy relationship fostered greater self-cohesion, self-esteem, and self-understanding in Anna. Anna experienced a more solid sense of herself in relation to her therapist as a female authority figure and a representative of the dominant white culture.

CO-TRANSFERENCE

An intersubjective systems perspective recognizes that it is impossible for two people in a therapeutic relationship to interact without influencing one another. Within an intersubjective system of reciprocal mutual influence, feelings traditionally labeled as transference and countertransference must arise. Both members of the dyad bring aspects of their biological and culturally embedded characteristics to the therapeutic process, and these features inevitably influence one another. Leary (2000) uses the term "racial enactments" (p. 641) to characterize interactions in which either participant's cultural attitudes emerge in some way. Leary (1997) describes the race of the therapist as an important kind of nonverbal self-disclosure that inevitably plays into treatment:

> Race and ethnicity—particularly when they are observable features of the analyst's self—represent a kind of self-disclosure. Although I have not conveyed anything in particular about myself, the fact that race is written on my face shapes the clinical dialogue to follow. While it is reasonable to argue that any of our particularities as individuals also represent disclosure of this kind, I believe that the valence of race may be of a different order in the present climate of the racial divide (p. 166).

In an intersubjective system, all verbal and nonverbal communications are expressions of the way both parties organize their experience, and inevitably aspects of both are revealed to the other (Kalb 2002). For example, it is not that the person is displacing or projecting some important relationship from the past onto the therapist, as traditional notions of transference suggest. Rather, the therapist becomes assimilated into the person's personal subjective world of experience (Stolorow and Lachmann 1984/1985). The same can be said for the therapist, whose feelings have traditionally been labeled as countertransference. To recognize the mutual construction of the experience of both, Orange (1995) prefers the term "co-transference."

The unique manner in which the meanings of race and ethnicity are assimilated into the subjective worlds of experience of both participants is understood as one aspect of their ongoing construction of experience. Since the two participants come together to make sense of one person's experience, the meaning of the therapist for the other is explored as a means of further understanding the other's organizing principles.

The therapist's gender and cultural heritage necessarily impact the therapy process; these characteristics of the therapist are part and parcel of the intersubjective field and are instrumental in evoking and shaping the clinical themes that emerge in the dialogue. The unique meanings that the person attributes to the therapist's race or ethnicity will depend on the person's own organization of experience. While race and ethnicity may not appear to be significant or pressing issues in a given therapeutic relationship, culture is necessarily always present, whether it is acknowledged consciously or unconsciously. The meanings both participants make of race and gender are influenced by the larger societal and cultural context in which racial and ethnic views of both participants have been formed, as well as the local culture of their unique family systems. Leary (2000) points out that race can be seen as a "complex negotiation within persons as well as a complex negotiation between persons" (p. 649).

Cultural heritage may have become an important organizer of experience for both members of the therapy dyad in such a way as to evoke a fear of repetition of painful or frightening experiences with members of the other's ethnic group. It would be socially reparative for both to understand and collaboratively articulate the historical contexts for the organization of this aspect of experience. In addition to the meanings that are made of the other's physical attributes, it is perhaps inevitable that in the course of meeting, statements that are reflective of biases will be unwittingly articulated. It is probably impossible to avoid such biases as "racism is built into the ways we think and speak, into the concepts and language on which we are socialized" (Altman 2000, p. 592). Leary (2000) points out that racial enactments in therapy offer a potential "to open up an important piece of clinical understanding or to derail the exchange if they are not effectively handled" (p. 642). This calls for a great degree of trust that must be earned by both participants. Experiences of rupture or intersubjective disjunction over cultural differences, while inevitable, can be turned to therapeutic advantage through reparative efforts. Relational and reparative actions that acknowledge and understand the other's humanity promote reconciliation.

CONCLUSION

Not only does the application of an intersubjective systems sensibility expand the range of emotional flexibility for both participants in the therapy, it also contributes to the promotion of social justice in psychology. To advance the aims of social justice, psychologists and psychoanalysts must push beyond the acceptance of diversity and work toward establishing "a more equitable distribution of power and resources so that all people can live with dignity, self-determination, and physical and psychological safety" (Goodman 2001, p. 4). To seek social justice means challenging prejudicial organizing principles so that our society as a whole begins to expand its receptivity to other worlds of experience. As Bucci (2002) cautions, "we need to broaden the application of psychoanalysis for the survival of our field, but also, I would argue, for the survival of our dissociated and potentially self-destructive species" (p. 225).

Exploration of the way in which the context of culture impacts subjectively organized worlds of experience can be a powerful mechanism of psychological growth. While a society entrenched in oppression is "clearly damaging to people in disadvantaged groups, it also requires people in advantaged groups to deny their own emotional capabilities, sensitivity, and mutuality. This stifles emotional honesty and hinders the development and use of empathy" (Goodman 2001, p. 107). An understanding of the way our relationships with our cultural context organizes our subjective worlds of experience has potentially positive applications beyond our dyadic systems approach to therapy and to a broader understanding of intercultural relations. As Altman (1995) put it, "If, as I suggest, defensive psychic functions are served by constructing these categories as we do, to think psychoanalytically about how we use social class, culture, and race, is to expand the range of our consciousness" (p. xvii).

Chapter Six

Prejudice as a Function
of Self-Organization

Coauthored with Martha Kendall Ryan, PsyD

Considering the degree to which racial, ethnic, and religious hatred permeate society, little psychoanalytic attention has been devoted to understanding and treating this social phenomenon. Perhaps this is because prejudiced attitudes, beliefs, and accompanying affects tend to be ego syntonic. Skinheads and neo-Nazis rarely seek out treatment for guilt or shame around their hateful ideologies. When we encounter prejudice in the consulting room, it is rarely as the presenting problem; rather, its presence is embedded in the person's overall self-organization.

Working with prejudiced people can be emotionally disturbing for therapists with humanistic values. Prejudiced people repeatedly confront their therapists with the repugnant attitudes, beliefs, and affect states that have infused their organization of experience. Maintaining a stance of sustained empathic inquiry in the face of powerful affective repugnance to prejudice is indeed a challenge for the therapist. One factor that can mitigate the disruptive effects of the therapist's affective reaction is a fuller understanding of the systemic meanings of prejudice for both participants.

Contributions to the psychoanalytic understanding of the phenomenon of prejudice come primarily from the ego psychology and Kleinian traditions. In this chapter, we will first review those psychodynamic and treatment formulations. We will then examine intersubjective systems theory's contribution to furthering the understanding of both the psychodynamic roots of prejudice and the therapeutic stance for promoting the unfolding, illumination, and transformation of prejudiced attitudes and affects. The treatment of Sandy, a woman with a history of failed occupational and interpersonal relationships, will be discussed to illustrate how prejudiced attitudes and affects may be manifestations of an underlying fragile and fragmentation-prone self-organization.

93

THE VIEWS OF EGO PSYCHOLOGY AND KLEINIAN THEORY

One familiar dynamic formulation for prejudice involves the defense of displacement (referred to as scapegoating in the social psychology literature). In this dynamic, the prejudiced person is thought to be displacing rage and aggression away from the true object of these affects, who could potentially retaliate against the subject in a damaging or destructive way, and onto individuals or groups who are perceived as weak and incapable of retaliation.

Another common dynamic formulation for prejudice involves the defense of projection. Psychoanalytic theory has identified two distinct uses of the construct of projection to explain prejudice. The first views projection as originating from within an ego-superego conflict, wherein the person's own harsh and critical superego demands are projected onto another group who are then seen as manipulative, demanding, and aggressive (Young-Bruehl 1996). The second treats the individual's prejudice as reflective of an id–ego conflict in which pressure from the id causes the projection of drive derivatives onto another group who may then be seen as "lecherous, sensuous, lazy at work, inferior—a fountain of instinctual drive" (Young-Bruehl 1996, p. 54). Laplanche and Pontalis (1973) combine both and note that "the racist . . . projects his own faults and unacknowledged inclinations on to the group he reviles." They refer to this as a "disowning projection" (p. 351).

Arlow (1994) proposes that prejudice, particularly toward the Jews, is a "psychodynamic constellation . . . a psychological predisposition associated with persistent unconscious fantasies, reactions to primitive, irrational, childhood wishes" (p. 284). The source of prejudice toward the Jews, Arlow suggests, is the blood libel myth. Persisting since the Middle Ages, this myth portrays Jews as murderous and cannibalistic toward non-Jews, particularly toward Christian children. Jews are seen as not quite human but appearing to be so by virtue of special powers. This denial of the essential humanity of the Jews has persisted, Arlow believes, because "it must resonate with some deep, primitive, unconscious wish, a kind of unconscious fantasy easily shared in common, based upon common need" (p. 288). This unconscious wish grows out of the desire of the older sibling to devour and replace the favored newborn who is now the object of his parents' undivided attention. "The blood libel accusation," Arlow writes, "originates from the projection of these infanticidal and cannibalistic wishes from the Christian upon the Jew" (p. 292).

Societal influences on the development of prejudice also have been recognized in the psychoanalytic literature. Referring to the work of Bettelheim, Szajnberg (1994) observed: "Prejudice is the precursor of acted-out aggression; it is the readiness to depersonalize individuals and treat them disdainfully, hatefully as a group. It is one of the hazards of a mass society" (pp. 491–92). Bettelheim's study of German soldiers who had just returned from World War I found that "intolerance was a function of perceived self-deprivation and anxiety about the future" (p. 492); the greater the person's anxiety, Bettelheim proposed, the more prejudiced he or she is.

The Kleinian construct of projective identification has also been used to explain the dynamics of prejudice. For example, according to Chatham (1996),

> A negative manifestation (of projective identification) would be pathological disavowal of one's own unacceptable images and feelings, such as Adolf Hitler's projection of his own defects onto the Jews. . . . Once Hitler projected onto the Jews, he could not bear to have them near him. He persecuted them and then began to fear that they would retaliate or contaminate him, thus leading to his systematic extermination of them (pp. 79–80).

These more traditional psychoanalytic perspectives on prejudice appear to cluster around two main ideas: the first involves a disavowal of the instinctual drives of aggression and sexuality (as in Arlow's description of the blood libel myth); the second concerns the management of anxiety over these impulses through the use of the defense mechanisms of projection, projective identification, and displacement.

THE DYNAMICS OF PREJUDICE FROM AN INTERSUBJECTIVE SYSTEMS PERSPECTIVE

Intersubjective systems theory, sharing some of the insights of self psychology, contributes an additional perspective on understanding and treating prejudice. Utilizing clinical material from the treatment of Sandy, a single woman thirty-three years old, we will develop an intersubjective systems understanding of the meaning and function of her prejudice and demonstrate how the empathic-introspective mode of treatment promoted the unfolding, illumination, and transformation of her prejudiced attitudes and hostile affects. In particular, we will illustrate how at the core of Sandy's prejudiced attitudes, beliefs, and affects lies a narcissistically vulnerable and fragmentation-prone self-organization. Her hateful beliefs and affects did not derive from the displacement or projection of instinctual aggression, but from a developmental history that promoted narcissistic vulnerability and injury and her reparative attempts to shore up her fragmenting self-organization.

We can identify five dynamic factors that play a part in Sandy's prejudiced attitudes and affects. The first dynamic is consistent with Kohut's (1972, 1977) conceptualization of narcissistic hate and rage as disintegration products of a self-organization fragmenting under stress or threat. In this vein, Wolf (1988) describes narcissistic rage as targeting those objects "who threaten or have damaged the self" (p. 78). In this dynamic, hate and rage are reactive to narcissistic injury. The second dynamic concerns the self-protective function that hate and rage serve in the maintenance of her self-organization by keeping potentially hurtful others at a distance.

Dynamics three, four, and five bear more directly on prejudice against or hate for an impersonal group. The third factor concerns another way that the expression of hate and rage serve to preserve her organization of experience. Rather than being strictly a disintegration product, Stolorow, Brandchaft, and Atwood (1987) hold that "rage and vengefulness in the wake of injuries can serve the purpose of revitalizing a crumbling but urgently needed sense of power and impactfulness" (p. 22). Reckling and Buirski (1996) discuss rage in abused children as "a derailment in the development of affect regulation and as an attempt to prevent further injury" (p. 87) as well as "an attempt to restore a sense of personal power and agency" (p. 87). In this context, hate and rage serve adaptive and reparative functions.

In addition to these reactive, adaptive, and reparative functions of Sandy's hate and rage, a fourth protective dynamic functions as an antidote to the overwhelmingly painful affects of shame and humiliation that she experienced whenever her core organizing principles—the sense of herself as defective and therefore deserving of abuse—were engaged in the present. According to Buirski and Monroe (2000), "The antidote function . . . serves a self-protective function. But instead of protection from unacceptable instinctual impulse, the antidote functions to protect the individual from painful disorganizing affects" (pp. 84–85).

A fifth dynamic playing a part in the formation of Sandy's prejudiced attitudes and affects was the narcissistic defense of devaluing others. Devaluation is a self-regulating process where self-esteem is elevated or enhanced not through merger with an idealized other but by feeling better than or superior to others. Both the antidote function and devaluation played an essential role in the construction of Sandy's prejudiced attitudes, beliefs, and affects.

THE CASE OF SANDY

The History

Sandy is a thirty-three-year-old Caucasian single female who lives alone. As a child, Sandy moved frequently due to her father's navy career and much of her early life was spent overseas. The result was a very insular childhood, punctuated by the nearly daily emotional and physical abuse visited on her by her father. Her mother, she recounted, ignored her complaints about the mistreatment and sided with her father against her. Sandy recalled that her brother "could do no wrong," while she felt incapable of pleasing her parents. The highly conflictual dynamic between Sandy and her parents took a more ominous turn in her early adolescence. She recalled that when she turned thirteen, her father's physical abuse became more sexual in nature and her appeals to her mother were met with accusations of Sandy's "flirtatiousness." Sandy believed her mother saw her as a sexual or romantic rival for her father's affections and therefore not only failed to protect Sandy from her father's abuse but also blamed her for provoking it. The early and unrelenting injuries Sandy suffered at the hands of her family culminated in her first and only psychotic break at the age of fourteen. She recalled experiencing auditory hallucinations wherein the angry voices of her parents shouted her name over and over as she writhed in her bed under blankets and pillows. She was hospitalized for six weeks in the state mental hospital, diagnosed with major depression and anorexia. In the next few years, with intermittent treatment via a variety of mental health center clinicians, Sandy's symptom presentation acquired the label Borderline Personality Disorder.

Sandy believed that her subsequent experience with the mental health system was largely unhelpful. She alternately expressed anger about having her personality cast as disordered and relief that this label offered her disability benefits including subsidized housing. She was transferred for a variety of reasons from one therapist to another within the mental health system responsible for her care, leading Sandy to conclude that she was "not able to be helped" and "so angry and difficult that every therapist kicked me out sooner or later." These abandonment experiences were a repetition of the abuse and rejection she was subjected to at the hands of her parents, where hopes for reparative experience ended in retraumatization.

No treatment with the many therapists Sandy encountered over her lifetime lasted for more than a few months. It is important to note that many of these therapists had imposed fairly strict limits on the vulgar, profane, and racist language of prejudice Sandy was permitted to use in the therapy room, the range of topics she was allowed to discuss, and the emotional tone she was to use toward her clinicians. Her experience of her therapists was, "I wasn't allowed to get angry at them." These therapists were impatient with her and may have felt predisposed in some way against her, perhaps because her hateful expressions stirred up difficult or conflicting feelings in them.

Since it is not uncommon to find therapists who view prejudice, like other attitudes and beliefs, as the outgrowth of a social and cognitive learning process, we want to digress for a moment to discuss the hurtful and counter-therapeutic effects of this stance. Such treatment approaches are designed to modify or change attitudes. For example, Sandhu and Aspy (1997) advocate that therapists be held accountable for challenging racist expression within the therapy hour. Such attempts to modify cognitions with people in individual treatment are well intentioned but ill conceived, and, we would argue, are doomed to fail the individual as well as the therapist's goals for society. While well intentioned, this proactive agenda-driven approach to a single aspect of the person's presentation inherently limits the person's open expression within the therapeutic relationship, confounds the purpose of therapy, and compromises its reparative potential. By "forbidding" the person's intolerance to unfold within the therapeutic relationship, the therapist effectively denies critical aspects of the person's self-experience. These approaches view prejudiced attitudes and affects as an isolated broken part that can be extirpated from the body as a whole, like removing the appendix, as opposed to viewing prejudice as a manifestation of a larger systemic problem.

As psychoanalytically oriented clinicians, we know that emotional growth does not result from trying to change the belief systems of those we work with through the imposition of our own. Such a feat, even if possible, would not represent a developmental transformation and a strengthening of self-cohesion. It would mean only that we had succeeded in pushing our "correct" beliefs onto someone whose lifelong compliance and pathological accommodation with the wishes of others has likely cost him or her much already.

It is not only misguided theoretical and technical approaches that can lead to therapists placing limits on the other's self-expression. When therapists feel themselves becoming disorganized or disregulated by the other's affective expressions of prejudice and hate, there is a tendency to blame and pathologize the person. Although such reactions serve transient affect regulating and self-organizing functions for the disrupted therapist, they unfortunately also lead to an escalation of hateful feelings in the other, setting up a reciprocally disregulating intersubjective field.

From the perspective of the person's subjective experience, having constraints placed on free expression, especially where the person may initially have been instructed to follow the cardinal rule of free association, could be experienced as the negation and invalidation of the person's self-organization. It can exacerbate the person's internal sense of disorganization, confirm expectations of abandonment, and be experienced as a retraumatization. To force its containment is to collude unwittingly with those whose lack of affect attunement, neglect, and abusive treatment led to the development of such rage and hatred in the first place. As we will see with Sandy, these experiences in her prior treatments proved to be replications of her early trauma, and she blamed herself for her therapists' empathic failures, just as she had her parents'. These treatments essentially reaffirmed her expectations of having her selfobject needs met with misattunement and faulty responsiveness. It is not at all surprising, then, that Sandy began yet another attempt at therapy in a highly conflicted and hypervigilant state, fully expecting at any moment to be rejected and punished for who she was and what she believed.

The Course of Treatment

The treatment we will describe was conducted by Martha Ryan, PsyD, and lasted two years. Sandy was a severely troubled person who had rarely encountered anyone in her life who promoted selfobject experience and she was filled with doubts and mistrust. Sandy brought to this treatment the fear that this new therapist, too, would abandon her, or worse, berate her for the person she felt she was exposing herself to be. Each time Sandy gave unbridled expression to her feelings and thoughts, she experienced a kind of elation resulting from her ability to share her internal life with an attuned other. However, this was usually followed by a period of extreme fear that she would be punished for the content and manner of her expression. One week the therapist might encounter a woman eager for self-revelation, and the next, an angry, sullen, glaring, childlike being, arms crossed, chair slowly edging back to the wall of the therapy room. Often her mood would vacillate within a single session.

The fact that Sandy was willing to continue therapy in spite of its painful nature, we believe, was directly due to those moments in which she had risked revealing herself and had felt accepted, affirmed, and understood. It was also due to her therapist's focus on repairing the inevitable disruptions to the treatment relationship that periodically occurred. This entailed exploring with Sandy the therapist's contribution to the shared intersubjective field that gave rise to her reactions. An example of how the therapist approached this was, "We seemed to be speaking freely until I asked you to tell me more about your response to your boss. I'm wondering if my asking made you feel criticized, and that is why it is hard for you to continue." Despite her mistrust and her expectation of retraumatization, Sandy's experience of being understood and accepted by her therapist promoted forward movement in the therapy. That this process was very slow speaks to the absence of affectively attuned caregivers in her environment for much of her young life.

Sandy's work experience was as spotty and marked with conflict and abrupt departures as her therapeutic and personal relationships. One indicator of progress in treatment came to be Sandy's ability to sustain employment for longer than a few months. When she first came to treatment, she had been employed as a nurse's aid for about two months by a private Jewish nursing

home. One of her goals was to work through the various interpersonal conflicts that had always disrupted her previous employment. She hoped that,
through this therapy, she could finally attain some economic independence
from her parents by keeping this job.

Even at age thirty-three, she continued to rely on her parents to fill the
monthly financial gaps left after her disability funds and sporadic paychecks
were spent. Frequent reminders that "you've always been a failure" accompanied their financial assistance. Sandy had a deeply embedded fear of losing
her tie to her parents, despite the painful experiences to which she felt subjected. At the beginning of treatment, Sandy stated with conviction that her
reliance on her parents was solely necessitated by her economic needs. Yet
this struggle was very much an alive concretization of her lifelong pursuit of
needed selfobject functions even in the face of repeated injury and disappointment. She often expressed confusion about why she continued to relate
to them at all but found any explanation other than money very difficult to examine until late in the therapy.

In the beginning phase of therapy, weeks passed in which Sandy continued
to express with surprise her sense that "these people at work seem nice, they
seem to like me." She noted that their Jewish faith was counter to her own
fundamentalist Christian beliefs but felt her experience there to be a positive
one. In a short time, however, Sandy began to be unhappy at work. At first,
her complaints about her supervisor and coworkers were unremarkable: "I
don't have enough responsibility," "I have too much responsibility, " "I don't
know if they like me," "They don't pay me enough," and so on.

At this time, therapy was focused on helping Sandy sustain a sense of herself as a valuable, worthwhile person who could contribute meaningfully to
the lives of the elderly with whom she came in contact. Her own childhood
experiences of feeling neglected, unwanted, and abandoned enabled her to
feel compassion for the elderly who seemed to be having a similar experience. She felt especially capable of helping them feel important, and treated
them with extra attention and warmth. This paralleled her own experience in
therapy, and she managed to avoid the significant absenteeism that threatened
her previous employment. Soon, however, her remarks began to take on a
more paranoid tone.

The increase in her paranoia can be linked directly to Sandy's archaic organization of experience. Her early sense of worthlessness developed in an intensely
harsh, rejecting, and painful family atmosphere. Sandy had to watch her brother
being treated as valuable, while she was a target of sexual, physical, and verbal
abuse by her father. Compounding this parental betrayal was her mother's rejection and invalidation of her. In this way, Sandy experienced her parents as col-
luding in a brutal negation and invalidation of her self-experience. To maintain

the crucial object tie with her primary caregivers, Sandy came to blame herself for the harsh treatment she received. Denying and disavowing the validity of her subjective experience of abuse and neglect, she concluded that she was defective and deserving of such treatment. This organizing principle was actively engaged in the present when Sandy interpreted any relational difficulty as evidence that she was inherently defective. Sandy's experience of championing the needs of the elderly in her care and her complementary experience of validation and attunement from her therapist facilitated her reexamination of her own experience of persecution as a child. She recalled not having anyone on her side when she was growing up, and began to wonder: "Why not? What was wrong with me that no one took my side?" She had come to therapy at first tentatively defending how "normal" her parents were: "They did the best they could with a kid like me." Over time, the positive connection she began to have with the elderly residents, coinciding with the developing attuned and validating selfobject relationship with her therapist, served to promote greater self-esteem and self-cohesion. As Sandy felt more integrated, the conviction that she was unworthy and to blame for the abuse she experienced began to diminish. What emerged was anger and rage at her parents. However, she was still not able to integrate this affect and it found symptomatic expression.

Sandy began to report absences from work due to a myriad of somatic complaints while still on probation as a new employee. She stated that by questioning the frequency of her illnesses her supervisors were giving evidence that they "are trying to get rid of me because I'm not Jewish, because I follow Christ." More and more, she felt like an outsider, persecuted for her Christian faith. She reported, for example, that "Jews only believe Jews and I'm not a Jew." Her therapist came to understand that Sandy's feeling of being persecuted was a concretization of her experience of having being unfairly and unjustly abused and blamed as a child.

As a series of Jewish holidays approached, Sandy felt her coworkers were whispering about her and "purposefully rubbing my nose in the fact that I'm Christian," by celebrating their holidays and not acknowledging hers. Her own family largely ignored religious rituals, and her family holidays were marked by obligatory and very uncomfortable encounters. Compared with the joyfulness of the nursing home staff and residents, Sandy's own deep sense of isolation came painfully to the surface.

To this point in the therapy, Sandy had generally oscillated between moments of understanding her employers' position regarding her absences and interpersonal difficulties and her belief that they were prejudiced against her. Now she moved to a more purely anti-Semitic expression, describing them as "vicious and vindictive" or "greedy people who only take care of their own." Her therapist's discomfort increased exponentially as Sandy's prejudicial statements became significantly more hostile and abusive. "I used to look at pictures of the Holocaust and cry. Now I understand why that happened to the Jews," Sandy began one session: "They are just horrible people; they deserved it, or God would have protected them." Through her hate for and devaluation of the Jews, Sandy offset her own feelings of shame and worthlessness. Her prejudicial statements escalated as her subjective sense of persecution increased: in this way, Sandy was attempting to shore up her fragmenting self-organization. In this example, we can see the operation of the antidote function and the function of devaluation. The understanding of these dynamic functions of Sandy's prejudice helped her therapist modulate her own discomfort.

The extreme damage done to Sandy had never been repaired; she had never had an opportunity to feel understood and so could not understand the source of her own hatred. Her therapist, therefore, tried to maintain a consistent stance of sustained affect attunement so as to promote the unfolding and illumination of Sandy's self-experience. Her therapist chose not to chastise her or negate her prejudicial statements. Instead, her therapist would acknowledge Sandy's experience of parental abuse as a way of explaining the distress that spawned her anti-Semitic beliefs. Following articulations like "It's so painful always to feel second best; you feel it now just as you did when you were young and your brother was favored," Sandy showed evidence of her growing sense of self-cohesion and capacity for self-observation when she reported: "Maybe some of it's me. . . . Well, sometimes maybe I have a part in it. I guess if I come to work in a bad place, looking for a fight, I have to figure they won't be nice to me." (Parenthetically, this series of interchanges illustrates how attunement to affect states and the validation of subjective experience do not reinforce narcissistic preoccupation, as learning theory might suggest. Rather, by promoting self-cohesion, self-understanding, and affect integration, the person becomes able to tolerate and acknowledge her own fallibility without evoking crushing feelings of shame and humiliation.) Sandy's therapist responded, "It makes sense that how you're feeling influences how you respond to them, especially since, given your history, you've come to expect that you'll be treated badly. It makes you question how people in the present will react to you, maybe puts you on guard before you have a chance to read them." Sandy's response to this and similar articulations suggested that she experienced her therapist as an attuned, understanding presence. Further, through the articulation of the operation of Sandy's core organizing principles, self-understanding and the transformation of self-experience were promoted (Buirski and Haglund 1999).

Understanding how Sandy's prejudiced attitudes grew out of her organization of experience and the operation of the five dynamic factors discussed above enabled her therapist to decenter from her personal discomfort with Sandy's hateful verbal expressions. In addition, affirming selfobject relationships with understanding professional colleagues also were sustaining and organizing. Thus, her therapist was able to maintain an attuned stance even when she found the content of Sandy's diatribes deeply disturbing.

Treatment Outcome

During the course of therapy, Sandy became more connected and comfortable in the therapeutic relationship. She sustained eye contact, nearly absent at first, for greater periods of time, often leaning forward in her chair, and she became more engaged in the therapy as a kind of dialogue. According to Orange (1995), "The nature of understanding is that alone we can come to understand only what we already understand. To risk testing our organizing principles in dialogue with a text or a person makes possible a new meaning" (p. 73).

As therapy progressed, Sandy integrated a more positive sense of herself as competent and courageous, particularly in the light of her personal history. She began to see herself as lovable within the context of her relationship with the elderly she cared for and was more able to hear and respond to praise than she was at the beginning of therapy. Regarding her feelings of persecution and their manifestation in anti-Semitic terms, Sandy developed more balance in her understanding of others, though when stressed she still tended to idealize or devalue others and was often confused by their motives. She also started to understand how her unpredictable, invasive, and traumatic childhood had influenced her affective responses and behavior in her adult relationships. This recognition helped her have more choices in the present, and she began moving into unfamiliar but more rewarding behaviors. She reported some measure of success in feeling more confident and appropriately assertive in her personal and professional relationships and exhibited improvement in these areas within the therapeutic relationship. She maintained her employment past the one-year mark in spite of her reported difficulties. An additional benefit of treatment for Sandy was her increasingly positive response to discussions of therapeutic misattunement as part of a two-way relationship of mutual recognition, rather than as a sign of imminent abandonment.

Sandy developed insight around her internal state when her distress was reflected in her angry statements about the Jews. Now when the therapist articulated Sandy's sense of herself as always second best, never good enough, Sandy responded: "It reminds me of being a child, and always compared against my brother, the prince, and I was just shit. It's just like that feeling." She then began to reframe her hatred as "It's not just the Jews, it's everybody," and further in the course of therapy: "It's just how much hatred I have from my childhood. It's not anybody else."

Sandy was becoming more conscious of the core principles that have organized her experience. Sustained affect attunement and the dialogue leading to greater self-understanding, as opposed to the limit setting and punitive approaches of her earlier therapy experiences, enabled Sandy to integrate her hateful feelings. As she was able to integrate her hateful affects, her prejudiced attitudes began to subside.

DISCUSSION

From the self psychologically informed intersubjective systems perspective, Sandy suffered from what she experienced as multiple interconnected narcissistic injuries: first, there was the physical and sexual abuse she endured at her father's hands; second, her mother's turning a blind eye to her father's sexual abuse; third, the failure of her mother to provide caring, attuned responsiveness to Sandy's feelings of hurt and betrayal by father; fourth, her mother's denying and invalidating Sandy's subjective experience of the abuse; and fifth, as discussed in chapter 7, there was no attuned witness to Sandy's suffering. Sandy's low self-esteem, unstable self-cohesion, susceptibility to fragmentation, and unintegrated affect states grew out of these chronic childhood experiences of misattunement and harsh and abusive treatment by her primary caretakers. While part of her longed for a selfobject relationship with her therapist that would be reparative, as seen in her persistent attempts to connect with a therapist, her fear of retraumatization through disappointment and rejection led her to form avoidant attachments.

In her current treatment, Sandy's profound fear of retraumatization emerged despite her therapist's efforts to remain consistently attuned. (This highlights how attunement is measured by the subjective experience of the person and not the best intentions of the therapist.) Sandy was mistrustful of her current therapist's efforts at attunement because she had the strong conviction that these efforts must be a ruse. She suspected that the therapist's motive was to feign understanding to exploit Sandy for the therapist's own ends. Sandy had been chronically unable to integrate the very painful feelings arising from the physically harsh and emotionally destructive parental environment of her childhood and adolescence. This resulted in the development of a reactive, self-protective antagonistic stance that prevented further traumatization but left her feeling as she did as a child: full of shame and self-hatred, unwanted and unworthy of praise, and unlovable. These became the crushing organizing principles of her self-development.

Morrison (1989) proposes that "[U]nderlying many expressions of rage is a feeling of shame—a feeling that reflects a sense of failure or inadequacy so intolerable that it leads to flailing out, an attempt to rid the self of the despised subjective experience" (pp. 13–14). Sandy's experience of early neglect at the hands of her mother and active shaming via the abuse of her father resulted in sensitivity to shame, wherein "the child, lacking a positive sense of self, readily reacts with shame to the inevitable slights and conflicts of childhood. . . . The earlier in development that shame-inducing interactions occur, the stronger will be the adult's predisposition to debilitating feelings of shame" (Morrison 1996, p. 60).

From Sandy's recollection of her formative history, we can understand why she felt hated, how she organized her experience around the beliefs that she was defective and deserving of abuse, and how her own feelings of hate resulted from such narcissistic injuries. Her expression of hatred took on a specific target when she identified it with some remnant of her earlier history, such as feeling like an outcast, feeling unappreciated or misunderstood. From this perspective, Sandy's prejudice served as an antidote to the painful affects of shame and self-loathing that surfaced when her organizing principles were engaged. Sandy's shame and self-loathing, which had coalesced out of her experience with grossly misattuned caregivers, were offset by feelings of righteous hatred and rage directed onto others whose stereotyped actions seemed to justify such prejudiced attitudes.

For Sandy, the hated group was the Jews, and she achieved a sense of belonging and self-worth by imagining herself to be a member of a righteous Christian community who were victimized by the powerful, greedy, scheming Jews. Sandy's sense of having deserved her parents' abuse was an organizing principle of her self-experience. It engendered in her a deeply felt sense of worthlessness and shame that was too painful for her to bear. She could not tolerate experiencing her coworkers as rejecting her because she was worthless and undeserving. She therefore came to understand it as persecution for a trait the larger society might find valuable—her Christianity (Arlow 1994). In Sandy's case, Christianity might also have served as the object of an idealized connection. According to Kohut (1971), Sandy could be understood as "forever searching for external omnipotent powers from whose support and approval . . . [she attempts] . . . to derive strength" (p. 84). Allying with the Christian majority, she could devalue an entire people who had their own history of horrendous abuse. Her belief that "the Jews deserved it" was both a devaluation that enhanced her own self-esteem and, in the words of Atwood and

Stolorow (1997), "a defensive grandiosity serving as an antidote to an underlying sense of defectiveness or deficiency" (p. 522). This defensive grandiosity, her sense that her Christianity provided her superiority over the devalued Jews, offset the deep sense of pain and alienation she endured from the belief that having been abused in childhood was a fate she deserved.

Sandy's choice of the Jews as the object of her prejudice seemed to derive from her situational context rather than some longstanding hatred of the Jews. In fact, in employment positions prior to her nursing home work, Sandy reported holding disdain for the ethnicities of those she worked with, particularly those whom she perceived had some power over her. This interchangeable, context-driven factor suggests that for Sandy, it is not the object of hate that is important but rather the function that prejudice serves in her self-organization.

By offsetting feelings of shame with righteous hatred and by inflating her own defensive grandiosity through comparison with the devalued other, Sandy was able to shore up her vulnerable self-organization against further fragmentation. In this light, the expression of prejudice is viewed as a striving for health, an attempt to preserve the threatened organization of experience, rather than as a manifestation of drive breakthrough or sadism.

In Sandy's case, we can see that her experience of her parents' persistent and unrepaired misattunement led to the development of hateful feelings and threatened to fragment a fragile self-cohesion. The experience of selfobject relatedness with her therapist/witness contributed to Sandy developing greater self-cohesion, which included a more positively colored self-concept and a greater capacity for affect regulation and integration. From this strengthened position, she was able to tolerate an examination of the meaning of her prejudice and the gradual integration of her hostile affects. According to Shane, Shane, and Gales (1997), "it is only when this traumatized self state can be understood in the context of a positive new experience with the other in the present is there potential for a new self state to evolve, encompassing a capacity for self-consolidation" (p. 110).

Chapter Seven

Bearing Witness to Trauma from an Intersubjective Systems Perspective: A Case Study

Coauthored with Erin Shrago, PsyD

The experience of trauma is as old as human existence. The recognition of the pathogenic impact of traumatic experience on the mind of the individual is as old as psychoanalysis. Historically, psychoanalytic studies began with an investigation into the origins of hysteria and quickly led to an appreciation of the role of trauma in the formation of the disorder (Breuer and Freud 1955 [1893–1895]). As Breuer and Freud observed, "our investigations reveal, for many, if not for most, hysterical symptoms, precipitating causes which can only be described as psychical traumas" (p. 6). In fact, we think it fair to say that Freud began his psychoanalytic career by treating what today we would call "post-traumatic stress disorder" or PTSD. Many of their original theoretical and clinical ideas are still found to be relevant by modern researchers (van der Kolk 2000).

The *Diagnostic and Statistical Manual of Mental Disorders*—Fourth Edition Text Revision (DSM-IV-TR) (American Psychiatric Association 2000) identifies the sequelae of PTSD and describes the debilitating symptoms that one can experience following a traumatic event. The DSM-IV-TR identifies the traumatic event as something that involves "actual or threatened death or serious injury, or a threat to the physical integrity of self or others" (p. 463). A person who experiences PTSD is likely to have experienced intense fear and a sense of helplessness. Part of this helplessness involves the recurrent and intrusive recollections of the overwhelming event, which includes images, thoughts, or perceptions. It might also be characterized by nightmares and flashbacks wherein the person feels as if they are re-experiencing the event. Persistent avoidance of stimuli associated with the trauma as well as the numbing of general responsiveness are also characteristic of PTSD. A person who is affected might also display an exaggerated startle response, sleep disturbance, hypervigilance, and difficulty concentrating.

Although the DSM-IV-TR's list of symptoms is comprehensive, it does not capture the psychological depth of a trauma and how it affects a person's self-organization. There is abundant research about the effects of trauma on one's psychological functioning and the impact it has on one's sense of safety in the world. There is also literature on how victims psychologically try to manage their traumatic experience. Specifically, Freud (1955a [1920]) identified the action of the "repetition compulsion," which described a person's unconscious inclination to repeat or recreate his prior experience despite it having been hurtful or disturbing. Ego psychologists viewed the repetition compulsion as an attempt to overcome the experience of helplessness through the gaining of mastery. The repetition compulsion notion has been misguidedly used as a highly controversial explanation for why women who have been raped are considerably more likely to be raped again when compared to their non-victimized peers. This blaming of the victim has unfortunately detracted from the public's perception of psychoanalysis.

Interest in the impact of trauma, including the newer recognition of "Acute Stress Disorder" seen in the DSM-IV-TR (p. 469), continues to be high. There has also been more recent recognition of how people become secondarily affected by witnessing the traumatic experiences of others. This concept is relatively recent but there is a growing literature that addresses it. There appears to be more momentum in this area since catastrophes such as the Oklahoma City bombing and the horrors of September 11th. In the wake of these and other terrorist attacks, people all across the nation and the world began to report experiences of fear, hypervigilance, and other symptoms such as sleep disturbance, flashbacks, and nightmares. All of the common PTSD symptoms were identified in not only the family members of victims, but in many of the first responders, like firefighters, policemen, and emergency medical personnel. Such powerful reactions cannot be underestimated, as those who were exposed to or directly witnessed these events have indeed experienced intense emotional responses.

For those in the helping professions who are on the "front lines" of disasters, the "first" responders are more vulnerable to powerful and disturbing emotional experiences. Whether they are firefighters, physicians, or humanitarian relief workers, the impact of witnessing the trauma suffered by others firsthand can be life-altering. Psychotherapists, on the other hand, would fall more in the category of "second" responders. As psychotherapists, we rarely witness the actual events or the immediate aftermath. However, we are in the unique position of bearing witness to the trauma of others in one of the most intimate of ways. We hear the victims' stories; we see the tears. Survivors bravely share their terrible stories, their ongoing fears, their sense of help-lessness, and the pain of re-experiencing the events in the remembering and telling. Not only do we listen to their words, we see the raw emotional wounds that plague them. It is not a distant story on the news, an article in the newspaper, or an interview on the radio. It is palpable and personal and can be deeply upsetting for the therapist/witness.

The role of the witness is complicated. While there are risks to the witness of becoming emotionally disorganized by the overwhelming affects of the sur-vivor, the very act of " witnessing" is critical. It is a vital aspect of the thera-peutic relationship that we hope to establish as well as a central part of the therapeutic action we hope to promote.

Several psychoanalysts, like Poland (2000), Ogden (2001), and Goldner (2004) comment on the witnessing function of the analyst. Orange (1995) identifies the important selfobject function provided by the therapist who is emotionally ready and available to be a witness to the traumas those we work with have suffered. According to Orange (1995), "The selfobject experience of witness (is) a special form of participation in the intersubjective field, makes the other's experience real and valid and important to that other" (p. 136). As Orange (2004) further observes, "Witness is more than a self-object function, it is an intersubjective process of realization that allows emergence of new kinds of self-experience" (p. 11). By this, Orange is de-scribing an important function of the therapist/witness in facilitating the trauma survivor's capacity to put words to their frightening story by recon-structing it in the safe and supportive presence of an attuned other. Through the experience of sharing with the witness, the trauma survivor can gain ac-cess to disavowed or unformulated aspects of the experience. In the inter-subjective field constructed with the particular therapist/witness, the survivor and witness together further the unfolding, illumination, and artic-ulation of the meaning of the traumatic experience. As Orange (1995) points out, this indicates "the thoroughly intersubjective character of self-knowledge" (p. 137).

There is both theoretical and clinical debate about what constitutes "trauma." If there is disagreement about the nature of trauma, then there is even more room for debate around the concept of "secondary or vicarious trauma." While space doesn't allow us to examine all sides of the "secondary trauma" debate, our aim is to introduce an intersubjective systems perspective to the discussion. First, we will review some of the literature on the concept of secondary or vicarious trauma.

Researchers and clinicians are paying increasing attention to the phenome-non of vicarious trauma and are seeking to better understand how vicarious traumatization occurs and why it ranges in its severity and occurrence across therapists. McCann and Pearlman (1990) recognized the personal impact that treating those who have been traumatized can have on the therapist. They coined the term "vicarious traumatization" in an effort to affirm the validity of therapists' experiences of being traumatized by exposure to the overwhelming affects suffered by the trauma victims with whom they worked. Pearlman and MacIan (1995) define vicarious traumatization as "the transformation that occurs within the therapist as a result of empathic engagement with clients' trauma experiences and their sequelae" (p. 558). Such engagement includes listening to graphic descriptions of horrific events, bearing witness to people's cruelty to one another, and witnessing and participating in traumatic reenactments (Pearlman and Saakvitne 1995).

Many research studies point to the interplay of various contextual factors that contribute to the emotional distress therapists experience in the intersubjective treatment field created by both participants. Pearlman and MacIan (1995) found that working with traumatized people can have disturbing effects on therapists that are qualitatively different from the emotional impact of working with non-traumatized people. Specifically, characteristics of therapists, such as their personal trauma history, gender, and personal stress level, may interact with exposure to the other's trauma material in a way that might instigate trauma-related symptoms in the therapist. Various empirical studies have evaluated how different traits and predispositions of therapists can contribute to vicarious traumatization. Schauben and Frazier (1995) assessed vicarious traumatization, disrupted schemas, PTSD symptoms, burnout, and coping in 118 female psychologists and 30 female rape crisis counselors. They queried participants in an effort to determine if they were experiencing vicarious traumatization. They found that having a greater number of trauma survivors in one's caseload was correlated with increased disruptions in one's beliefs or schemas, with PTSD symptoms, and with the likelihood that one would report vicarious traumatization.

Studies on the reactions to rape survivors by researchers, emergency workers, and hospital staff, have also found that they manifest similar responses to those who have had direct traumatic experience (Genest, Levine, Ramsden, and Swanson 1990; Lyon 1993). Follette, Polusny, and Milbeck (1994) studied what they identified as "secondary traumatization" among 225 mental health professionals and 46 law enforcement officers who were providing services to survivors of childhood sexual abuse. These researchers evaluated the relations among the respondent's own childhood abuse history, current personal stressors, current PTSD symptoms, and current coping strategies. The study concluded that for law enforcement officers, personal stress, personal trauma history, and negative responses to investigating sexual abuse cases were predictive of trauma symptoms. The results from this study also indicate that the stress that therapists report as part of their personal lives and the strategies they use to cope with stress both in and out of session is related to the trauma symptoms they report.

A study conducted by Kassam-Adams (1994) reported findings from a survey of 100 psychotherapists. Her results indicated that therapists' exposure to sexually traumatized clients was directly related to those therapists showing symptoms of PTSD. In her particular sample of therapists (75% of whom were women), female gender, personal history of trauma, and exposure all contributed significantly to the prediction of PTSD symptoms. Another empirical study (Pearlman and MacIan 1995) showed that trauma therapists with a personal trauma history showed more negative effects from the work than those without a personal history. Interestingly, people who have experienced their own personal trauma are more likely to specialize in the treatment of trauma. However, working with traumatized people also impacted the self-esteem of those therapists with no prior personal trauma history. This study also identified a particularly vulnerable group of therapists, the beginning therapist.

Research has begun to identify the intersubjective and contextual factors that foster the susceptibility of beginning therapists to the disorganizing effects trauma narratives have on them. The beginning therapists in the sample experienced the most difficulties. Neumann and Gamble (1995), who evaluated countertransference and vicarious traumatization in the new trauma therapist, recognized that beginning therapists are especially vulnerable to experiencing secondary PTSD symptoms. Exploration of this topic has revealed that the trauma therapist whose identity is built around her work is particularly vulnerable to being secondarily traumatized. This might be manifested in disruptions in personal identity, self-cohesion, self-esteem, and agency. The beginning therapist has an increased likelihood of experiencing intrusive imagery of the traumatic incident, in particular, as well as a profound sense of professional incompetence. Saakvitne, Pearlman, et al. (1996) also recognize the power of intrusive imagery experienced by the therapist. Images may come during the day, during sex, or in nightmares. They report that images might be visual/auditory experiences, bodily sensations, smells, or emotional responses to certain cues.

To date, there has been little discussion of how the experience of bearing witness to trauma can affect the therapeutic dyad. If both participants are undeniably experiencing their own subjective distress, what is the impact on the relationship and the treatment? The intersubjective systems perspective, with its attention to the dyadic system, the relational and contextual construction of self-experience, and the interactive regulation of affects in the dyad (Beebe and Lachmann 2002), is an especially suitable perspective to apply to understanding the fate of disturbing affects and emotional distress in both participants.

Our worlds of affective experience become subjectively organized into patterns. The patterns or organizing principles may be described as the emotional conclusions that a person derives from lifelong experiences in their emotional environment, particularly those experiences in the early relationships with primary caregivers (Orange, Atwood, and Stolorow 1997). Therefore, one's organizing principles emerge from the intersubjective field of early child–caregiver relationships. A critical determinant of the quality of the child's early relational environment is the caregiver's capacity to regulate, modulate, and integrate aspects of the child's emotional experience. Stable self-organizations are promoted and consolidated by those selfobject experiences that further the regulation and integration of affective experience (Buirski and Haglund 2001). Conversely, experiences that shame, blame, and invalidate the child serve to undermine the developmental capacity to integrate and regulate painful or disruptive affect states, leaving the child vulnerable to self-fragmentation.

Intersubjective systems theory expands on the emphasis on subjectivity and the centrality of affect by identifying affectivity as the primary organizer of self-experience. From the intersubjective systems perspective, affective experience is at the core of the way experience is organized. Because of the central, organizing role of affective experience, recognizing, illuminating, exploring, and integrating affects become critical in developing new organizations of experience, or "organizing principles" (Buirski and Haglund 2001). Identifying and articulating the person's affect states illuminates both the person's formative early life experience as well as his or her current experience within the therapeutic relationship.

Therapeutic progress might be viewed as the process of supplanting old organizing principles with new ones that are formed in the context of an attuned selfobject relationship with the therapist. The task of therapy may be viewed as the effort to promote the unfolding, illumination, and transformation of affective experience (Stolorow, Brandchaft, and Atwood 1987). The intersubjective field formed by the therapeutic pair provides a developmental second chance by exploring, identifying, and articulating the person's subjective world of experience within the safety of an attuned selfobject relationship (Orange 1995). Out of this second chance new and more flexible organizing principles can emerge that expand and enrich the person's experience (Orange, Atwood, and Stolorow 1997).

In the remainder of this chapter, we will describe how the therapist's bearing witness to the other's trauma may play out in the intersubjective field created by the dyad. Additionally, we will specifically address how the therapeutic relationship and the therapist's self-disclosure of emotional distress can promote growth and mastery in both participants. We intend this as a contribution to the literature on the interplay of the subjective experiences of trauma on the two participants and the meanings the parties make of it within their therapy relationship. This exploration is a perfect fit with the intersubjective systems perspective, which addresses just that—the intersecting worlds of subjective experience in the members of the therapeutic dyad.

Keeping in mind that the intersubjective systems perspective focuses on the recognition, articulation, and illumination of the person's world of subjective experience as it emerges in the context of the therapeutic relationship, how do we reconcile this experiential, contextual emphasis with attempts to objectively define the state of trauma, like those found in the DSM-IV-TR? From the intersubjective systems perspective, trauma cannot be defined by reference to the particular event. It is not the event itself, however upsetting it might be, that is traumatic. Rather, it is the person's subjective experience of overwhelming affect in the face of a devastating event that characterizes the experience as traumatic. In the review of a clinical case of a traumatized person, Stolorow, Atwood, and Orange (2002) make the point that "the essence of psychological trauma lay in the experience of unbearable affect" (p. 125).

Furthermore, as Stolorow and Atwood (1992) point out, the traumatic consequence of the experience of overwhelming affect reflects the failure of the selfobject surround to attune to the victim's experience. Thus, there are several critical contextual variables that contribute to an experience resulting in traumatically overwhelming affect. In particular, the presence of attuned, non-judgmental, and accepting others can mitigate the degree to which painful affects aroused by an event will be experienced as overwhelming. This is an important distinction in that it emphasizes that trauma does not refer to the event, but to the relational context within which the event is experienced. What might be experienced as traumatic by one person might not be by another. One person might experience post-traumatic stress symptoms for months to years following a car accident, while another person's healing might end after the whiplash subsides. As we pointed out above, one of the DSM-IV-TR criteria for trauma is exposure to a life-threatening circumstance. However, for one soldier, being shot at might be an experience of overwhelming disturbing affect, while for another it might be a moment of exhilaration. Being shot at may or may not be traumatic; the critical determinant is the subjective experience formed within a specific relational context and its assimilation into the ongoing organization of experience that will determine the emotional meanings that the event has for the soldier.

Just as we can understand how a person's experience of unbearable or overwhelming affects in the absence of an attuned selfobject relationship may be traumatic, so we can appreciate how emotional distress can be aroused in the therapist by the impact of witnessing these affect states in the other. However, since we are defining trauma as the experience of overwhelming affect, no matter how disturbed the therapist might be by bearing witness to the other's traumatic experience, the distance from the immediacy of the experience suggests that the intensity of the therapist's affect state will rarely match the level of unbearable or overwhelming. Therefore, even though constructs like "vicarious" or "secondary" trauma sound compelling and descriptive, the therapist's experience is necessarily different from the victim's. Terms like "vicarious" or "secondary" trauma, suggest that the therapist has contracted something from the victim. Such "affect contagion," where, by analogy to infectious diseases, two people may pass a virus between them, are one-person, isolated-mind constructs. Affective experience is not spread by contact with and exposure to the distress of another, but is a co-constructed, emergent property of the intersubjective field. The therapist's emotional distress is necessarily shaped by both contact with the victim's emotional experience and her or his own history, creating unique meanings for the therapist.

We will now describe the treatment of Mary, a young woman who suffered overwhelming affects when brutally attacked, and the impact that bearing witness to Mary's experience had for both Mary and her female therapist.

Mary is a Caucasian, heterosexual female who came into treatment when she was twenty-five years old, after being referred by an academic advisor who encouraged her to seek help. Mary had disclosed to her advisor that she had been brutally attacked when she wouldn't surrender her money to a mugger. She had difficulty concentrating and hadn't been sleeping much since the incident. During the first several months of therapy, Mary was incredibly soft-spoken and had a timid demeanor about her that reflected her feeling of vulnerability. Mary appeared notably depressed, often sitting in a slumped-over position, making minimal eye contact. During the initial months of therapy, Mary spoke with difficulty, struggling to articulate her feelings. She frequently shrugged in response to inquiries and appeared detached with little insight into her problems. Mary demonstrated very little energy or animation in session and often responded in a sluggish manner. She reported significant sleep disturbance, characterized by recurrent nightmares and chronic anxiety. Mary did manage to convey that her level of functioning had been substantially diminishing since the assault.

Prior to the mugging, Mary had been a full-time graduate student on a scholarship pursuing a career in the arts. In addition to being a full-time student, she also maintained part-time employment at a retail store. Mary had been financially independent and lived in an apartment on her own. She was highly motivated and self-sufficient. After the assault, Mary stopped attending classes consistently, did not maintain her employment, and had to move out of her apartment due to her inability to pay rent. At that time, Mary moved in with her mother and younger sister, feeling that she had no other option.

Although Mary's initial reason for entering treatment was related to the physical attack, there were several other emotional issues that were troubling to her. Mary's mother was a substance abuser who had actively abused prescription medication for as long as Mary could remember. Mary also described being exposed to repeated domestic violence between her mother and father. She recalled instances of escalated verbal arguments as well as physical altercations between family members. Mary did not recall ever being the direct victim of any such physical abuse. However, she witnessed the physical abuse of family members and the intensified affects of fear and distress aroused by the violence around her. Since Mary's mother was herself overwhelmed by the father's attacks, she was unavailable to provide the needed selfobject functions of modulating and regulating Mary's own affect arousal. This, then, was part of the emotional context that contributed to the vulnerability of Mary's self-organization prior to the mugging.

It became clear throughout treatment that Mary had actually been quite "invisible" to others while growing up. It emerged in the therapy dialogue that Mary's tendency to be passive, submissive, and "invisible," was an effort to protect herself from her abusive surroundings. Mary's family members were emotionally neglectful and she often reported feeling "disposable" and unimportant. Her mother, in particular, was cold, distant, and self-absorbed. Her mother often placed her own needs before Mary's, including her pattern of "choosing" her husband over Mary. In addition, Mary's mother often spent what money she had on drugs and ignored Mary's need for financial assistance. As a child, because of the threats and invalidation by her parents, Mary had to disavow or disconnect from her own feeling states. She could not recognize, put words to, or appreciate the subjective validity of her affect states. Because of this history, much of Mary's treatment involved the process of identifying, articulating, and validating Mary's emotional experiences. Therapy became a place where Mary could work through her developmental longings for a selfobject relationship that would allow her to begin to acknowledge and integrate the frightening affects from her childhood and also from her recent experience.

Mary's history of caregiver misattunements, her emotional abandonment, and the feelings of betrayal of her trust served as an important backdrop for her subsequent traumatic experience. As Lachmann and Beebe (1997) describe, in a traumatic experience, like the one Mary experienced, "unconscious organizing principles and fantasies amplify the affects evoked and contribute to the overall impact of the event. Here unconscious elaborations of an event contribute to its traumatic impact . . . trauma derives its power from braiding together preexisting, less well-organized themes" (p. 279).

Mary was mugged following a social event at a downtown bar. Within seconds after her departure from the bar, Mary's life was endangered. She was attacked in the parking lot behind the establishment, an arm wrapped around her neck before she even recognized what was occurring. Her attacker's voice was in her ear, repeatedly saying, "Shut up." Mary vividly recalled the sensation of his heavy breathing in her ear and the odor of alcohol on his breath. Mary's descriptions of the event in treatment revealed how physically and emotionally overpowered she felt. Mary's attacker groped at her body, feeling for any valuables that he might want, and ultimately forcibly took her purse. During this assault, the attacker made sexual comments about her body, frightening Mary with the expectation that she would be raped. As she later articulated in therapy, he took from Mary much more than her purse. He took her safety and a part of her self. When the attacker was finished with her, he fled, leaving Mary feeling completely powerless and emotionally overwhelmed. What remained were the thumbprint bruises on Mary's arm and the red marks on her neck. The attacker also left a fragmenting and disorganized self-organization in his wake.

Considering Mary's history of witnessing violence in her family, her experience of being invisible, unrecognized, and disposable, the assault had a profound impact on her self-organization. In her mind, Mary's sense of inferiority and low self-worth originating from her childhood was confirmed by the abuse. She had not been listened to or seen, her objections violently overpowered, and she had suffered being devalued and used. Consistent with her prior organization of experience, Mary had made sense of this new assault as occurring because of something that she had done wrong. She had not fought back or called out for help to those nearby. She frequently berated and disparaged herself by saying, "I should have known better than to walk to my car alone."

Assimilating this assault into her ongoing organization of experience, Mary believed that she got what she deserved for being so "stupid." She concluded that she could have prevented the attack if she had walked with a friend, called a cab, not worn a purse, etc. Prior to beginning therapy and even for some time during therapy, Mary struggled with self-blame and criticism, with minimal recognition that she had been victimized. The assault actually lent confirmation to her organization of experience that she was not worthwhile, had no voice, and did not matter to people. The people in Mary's life had actively or consistently reinforced these self-depreciating beliefs. Sadly, there was no one to bear witness to her mistreatment, no one who disconfirmed or depathologized the meanings she made of her experience.

During the two and a half years of her therapy, Mary demonstrated many changes. Most notable was her ability to engage with her therapist in a trusting and forthcoming manner. During the initial months of treatment, her organizing principles emerged in her concrete and self-deprecating remarks when her therapist tried to attune to her affect and reflect her subjective experience. A typical exchange can be captured in the following dialogue when Mary would present a negative interaction with her mother.

Therapist: You feel like you're an inconvenience to her when you ask her for money, like you are a burden.

Mary: I don't know.

Therapist: It's like she doesn't see how hard you are working in school.

Mary: It doesn't matter anyway.

This brief exchange is representative of the first few months of therapy. Despite efforts to articulate and illuminate her experience and the associated affect, Mary did not experience her therapist as attuned. Rather, she clung to the familiarity and security of her organization of experience, by discounting, negating, or disavowing her own feelings and dismissing her therapist's efforts at attunement. This reflects how deeply one's organization of experience is entrenched and the great effort that goes into maintaining it. That is, even when exposed to someone trying to be an attuned and affirming figure, a person might still not recognize or allow this new, longed for relationship to enter into her experience. As a result, it took many months to establish a selfobject relationship wherein Mary could allow herself to accept being attuned to by another person, an experience that was incongruent with her organizing principle of being "invisible" and "worthless."

As Buirski and Haglund (2001) have noted, attunement is not something that the therapist can claim. It falls to the subjective experience of the other to assess whether or not she has experienced such attunement. However, in situations like that presented by Mary, people who have been consistently invalidated and misattuned to, and who have organized their experience around feeling undeserving of attunement, may be initially unable to tolerate or accept the attunement efforts of the other. Being attuned to is so at variance with the way their experience has been organized that it cannot be integrated or assimilated. Efforts at attunement are experienced as disorganizing because they contradict the way one has historically viewed the world and one's place in it. Rather than be able to reorganize or make new sense of one's experience in the world, interactions that disconfirm the existing organization of experience are dismissed or discredited. In this situation, Mary either just ignored her therapist's efforts at attunement or questioned the therapist's motives, as in "You are just taking my side because I pay you."

Mary's tendency to discount and disregard her own feelings could be seen across contexts and relationships, again suggesting a deeply entrenched organizing principle. A discussion about her disappointment when she did not get a job she had applied for revealed the same self-negation of her subjective experience.

Mary: I really don't have a choice (but to live with her mother)—I'm screwed all the way around 'cause I can't get another job.

Therapist: It's like there's no way out.

Mary: It could be a lot worse and I feel stupid 'cause I'm upset about it.

Therapist: You feel like you should just be able to deal with it?

Mary: Yes. I should.

Therapist: It's pretty hard to deal with all of this after you've worked so hard to be on your own. You've put so much effort into this. This is a huge disappointment (not getting the job). *Pause.* Does it feel like people understand how devastating this is for you?

Mary: My brother and mother know about it.

Therapist: Do they get it? How about your mother?

Mary: She didn't say anything. She just said, "You know how people mess up."

Therapist: It was just that simple, huh? Makes it feel like it's not a huge deal.

Mary: Yeah, like I'm not important.

This dialogue illustrates how the emotional misattunement from Mary's early caregiving relationships had been assimilated into her organization of self-experience. Despite her continued experience of invalidation, Mary was slowly coming to verbalize her organizing principle of not being important. This reflects the beginning of the unfolding and illumination of her subjective experience, although she was not yet fully ready to accept it as valid. She slowly became more verbal and began to establish intermittent and brief eye-contact that later developed into a comfortable and appropriate gaze. In contrast to her previous statements of self-invalidation, Mary gradually began to acknowledge and articulate her own previously disavowed affective states. In the presence of her therapist, the two were able to construct her subjective experience of events and together they put words to Mary's disappointment, frustration, and betrayal. An example of this came when Mary expressed annoyance with her mother's volatile moods and lack of emotional support. Following her continued efforts to assert her feelings, she expressed her irritation:

Mary: It is just ridiculous how moody she is!

Therapist: You sound incredibly frustrated and discouraged.

Mary: I am. Why can't she just support me?

Simple comments such as these reflect Mary's increased ability to recognize and acknowledge her affect and respect her own experience. She became less inclined to organize her experience around the old feeling that she deserved to be mistreated. In contrast, she was becoming more assertive about injustices she had suffered. Rather than attributing negative events to faults of her own, she began to attribute responsibility to others. Mary began to generalize her new organizations of experience in other situations and relationships as well. She began to see the violence that she had suffered as separate from her self-worth. In contrast to her previous tendency to see people's mistreatment of her as reflections of her own inadequacies, Mary began to feel stronger and more worthy. She began to recognize people who had unjustly mistreated her over the years, whereas she had previously never questioned their behavior toward her because it fit in with the way she had organized her experience; that is, she deserved whatever mistreatment came to her. A change in the way she organized her experience began to emerge in her rejections of her mother's devaluing comments:

Mary: Yeah, she finally said, "I'm so glad you're leaving" and I was like thanks, I love you, too.

Therapist: That's a really hurtful thing for her to say.

Mary: She was being a jerk yesterday but . . .

Therapist: That reminds me of that comment she said a long time ago . . .

Mary: Uh-huh. Yeah, 'cause I always tell her I know you're going to be glad when I'm gone and she says "No, that's not the point" but this time she just straight up and said it. So, I said thanks (sarcastically).

While Mary did not elaborate on the impact of her mother's statement toward her, it was not seen as avoidant. Rather, she had identified and processed much of the affect surrounding her relationship with her mother at this point in treatment and had made the shift of placing responsibility on her mother as opposed to her previous pattern of feeling the criticism was deserved. Her ability to recognize her mother's failings exemplified Mary's growing ability to acknowledge that there was not something inherently wrong with her. Mary had begun to see herself as mistreated by her mother because of her mother's own problems with addiction and selfishness.

Finally, the shift in Mary's self-critical organizing principles was seen in the reorganization of her subjective experience of the assault. She finally came to view herself as the victim of a crime, with a decreased amount of shame and self-blame attached to the experience.

Therapist: You didn't deserve what happened to you.

Mary: It's just not fair that I will be affected for the rest of my life and he won't think twice about what he did.

Therapist: He pays no consequences and yet you feel forever changed.

This exchange suggests the sadness that Mary was experiencing and her sense of being defeated by her attacker, but it also exemplifies her recognition of her affect and her subjective experience of having been violated. Her statements reflect the progress in her ability to articulate her increasing self-delineation and validate what she had and would continue to go through. She was no longer responding, "It doesn't matter." Her experience did matter. It was clear to her that it mattered to her therapist and most importantly, it mattered to Mary.

By the conclusion of treatment, the therapist no longer had to be the more verbal one. Rather, the therapist found herself trying to interject during Mary's animated and emotion-filled stories. When treatment began, Mary seemed to not want to reveal herself out of the expectation that she would be criticized. As the therapy relationship developed, Mary had lots to say. By the end of treatment, her stories and disclosures had a new flavor, a flavor of the future. Mary spent most of the final sessions talking about future-oriented goals. She no longer saw herself as a helpless victim, but rather regained her identity as a capable and gifted student with amazing resilience and potential. Times of self-doubt and disappointment remained, which Mary realized she was prone to because of her childhood environment. However, she had more internal resources to counteract them.

Early caregiving relationships become particularly relevant in the clinical context as people reveal and disclose their experience of these relationships.

Mary, like many other people that present for treatment, had experienced relationships involving massive misattunement and invalidation of her central affect states. This became particularly apparent in her relationship with her mother who did not recognize, attune to, or accept Mary's subjective experience and her associated affects. Her mother displayed a consistent narcissistic self-preoccupation that limited her ability to meet any of her daughter's emotional needs. Such consistent misattunement to Mary's basic needs left Mary more vulnerable to painful affect states, with less of an ability to soothe herself and regulate her affects. Additionally, the history of misattunement and invalidation Mary experienced structured the formation of her "organizing principles" such that she formed the conviction that her feelings did not matter, or even exist. Neglect was one of the many forms of invalidation that Mary experienced. There were, in addition, overt comments that negated or dismissed her feelings entirely. As a result of these early experiences, Mary's self-organization was primed for the experience of overwhelming and painful affect aroused by her assault, making the assault "traumatic" for her.

Zeddies (2000) emphasizes the destructiveness of caregiver misattunement when he explains that people have difficulty being "reflective about and accepting of their psychological and emotional experience, particularly if their lives have been shaped by people who were neglectful or antagonistic to helping them express and understand themselves" (p. 7). One of the important selfobject functions of the therapist's bearing witness that is so essential in facilitating the transformation of the other's subjective world of experience is the therapist's capacity to non-critically hear, tolerate, and contain the depth of the other's pain. Therapists are not detached, objective observers of another's life. The empathic/introspective stance of the therapist inevitably means that bearing witness also involves assimilating the victim's horrors into the therapist's organization of experience.

Another important, but no doubt controversial aspect of bearing witness concerns the therapist's openness to self-disclosing to the other the emotional impact on her of bearing witness to the victim's trauma. This self-disclosure of the affective experience of bearing witness to another's trauma is an additional selfobject function of bearing witness. This sense of "bearing" witness, which includes the notion of the therapist as one who "testifies," is fully intersubjective. This contrasts with Poland's (2000) notion of "being" a silent witness, a one-person formulation of therapist as observer. It is in this context that we will discuss how the therapist's self-disclosure of her subjective experience of Mary's trauma contributed to the consolidation of Mary's self-experience.

Mary's therapist was a graduate student with very limited clinical experience. She was filled with naive optimism, believing that therapy was a unidirectional service that she would provide. She identified herself as the "professional" in the room, not as the other person in the relationship. She never anticipated the impact that the trauma of the other would have on her, both professionally and personally. As a beginning therapist, she was unfamiliar with the research on the novice therapist's susceptibility to becoming disorganized by exposure to the traumatic experiences of others. Mary's therapist's vulnerability did not come from any prior history of personal victimization. Rather, it seemed to originate from her novice status as well as the repeated exposure to abuse cases she encountered as a first-year graduate student.

The therapist reported,

When I began to work with Mary, I could not deny the disturbing impact of her words on me. I heard her story of being violated and abused and the details of the physical and emotional assault. One of the first changes I recognized in myself was my sudden awareness of the terrors of the dark. Nighttime became a frightening and vulnerable time for me, particularly as I had to move from my car to the back door of my house. The short distance of about twenty feet felt like a mile. I was plagued with the thought of what could potentially happen in that twenty-feet transition from the dark to the comforts of my home. I, too, could be forever changed by a mugger hiding in the nearby trees or a stalker awaiting my arrival home. I was in no way protected from or invulnerable to the dangers of the dark. I also was aware of my racing pulse on my journey to the back door and my immediate action of locking the door after my entry. Even after I had secured the door, however, I did not feel safe. There was a lingering suspicion that I could be harmed at any time. My vigilance and anxiety were heightened, my startle response exaggerated.

The therapist noted other changes in her self-experience:

The once-welcomed respite of sleep turned into foreboding. I recall especially disturbing dreams wherein I became the protagonist in the trauma narrative I had heard from Mary. I was the one being victimized, with a level of detail and vividness I had never experienced. I had two nightmares that haunted me with their realism: I was being physically hit and overpowered by a perpetrator. Fortunately, as my work with Mary continued, these symptoms subsided within a short time. The security of my sleep returned. My racing pulse also decreased and I was able to transition from my car to the back door with less dread of "what if?" I noticed the changes in my subjective experience over the course of my work with Mary, ranging from feeling overwhelmed and frightened to feeling angry and empowered. The question that remained was what to do with these powerful feelings. I began to evaluate both the personal and professional aspects of these experiences and I began to consider whether self-disclosure could be helpful or harmful to Mary.

Why did the therapist's distress subside more easily than Mary's? This might be explained by several factors. First, while she found Mary's description of her assault disruptive and disturbing, she was a witness at a distance. Second, the therapist had the support of attuned and validating friends, colleagues, and supervisors with whom she was able to consult. Third, since the therapist did not have an abusive upbringing, she did not experience the same history of repetitive misattunements that Mary had experienced as a child. The therapist's self-organization was not vulnerable to becoming disorganized by overwhelming affect because of a prior history of unmodulated, unregulated, and unintegrated affects. She was able to identify and articulate her affective states and was therefore able to seek the support from friends and fellow professionals that she so needed.

As has been acknowledged earlier, there are a variety of theoretical perspectives that invoke the concept of intersubjectivity. For Stolorow and his collaborators, intersubjectivity refers to an overarching field or systems view concerning the contextual shaping of relationship. For American relational theorists, intersubjectivity can refer to a developmental achievement (Stern 1985) or a condition of the person's awareness of the subjectivity of the therapist (Benjamin 1995a, 1995b). These differing perspectives on intersubjectivity also carry with them different emphases on the role of the therapist's self-disclosure.

Central to both the intersubjective systems perspective and relational theory is the recognition of the two-person, co-constructivist activities of the therapeutic dyad. While intersubjective systems theory focuses on "the dialogic attempt of two people to understand one person's organization of emotional experience" (Orange 1995, p. 8), some relational theorists see intersubjectivity as going beyond the therapist's awareness to recommendations for the therapist to be more openly expressive and self-disclosing.

There is a growing literature on therapist self-disclosure. Aron (1996) provides an extensive discussion of the unfolding of the psychoanalytic debate on self-disclosure from Freud through the American relationalists. Teicholz (2001), coming at self-disclosure from the self psychological perspective, defines self disclosure as the therapist's "conveyance of information to the patient about any aspect of the analyst's life experience, in or out of the treatment relationship" (p. 11). Self-disclosure can be either intentional or inadvertent communication on the part of the therapist. However, as Aron (1996) observed, "self-revelation is not an option: it is an inevitability. Patients accurately and intuitively read into their analysts' interpretations the analysts' hidden communications" (p. 84). Teicholz (2001) also explained that "what is critical to the curative potential of any intervention is not whether it involves the analyst's self-containment or self-expression, but whether or not the patient can make use of it as a needed selfobject experience" (p. 19). This is why the therapist's self-expression should be approached with careful clinical judgment. Since each intersubjective field is unique, there can be no uniform technical recommendations about therapist self-disclosure (Orange and Stolorow 1998). What might promote one person's integration of affective experience might disorganize another. However, as treatment progresses and the therapeutic relationship evolves, we might develop a sense of whether some relevant piece of therapist self-disclosure could serve needed selfobject functions for this specific person. The emphasis on whether the person can make use of the therapist's self-disclosure as a selfobject experience is critical (Goldstein 1994). Therefore, in Mary's treatment, it was important to evaluate whether the therapist's self-disclosure of her subjective experience of distress and disorganization might provide needed selfobject functions for Mary that could not be provided in other ways.

Aron (1996) refers to the importance of the "mutual generation of data," in which the therapist shares his or her "associations with the other when those associations provide data that are absent from and yet directly relevant to the other's association" (p. 97). Pearlman and Saakvitne (1995) address the notion of a "shared discovery" (p. 18) between the two participants, wherein we move away from a position of authoritative knowing of the other to a more collaborative and mutual endeavor. These authors elaborate on this position in saying that "therapy will be unique for the interaction between the person of client and the person of therapist; the therapist's self is elemental to the unfolding therapeutic relationship" (p. 18).

The literature emphasizes the importance of such sensitivity as well as timing of a therapist's self-disclosure. Teicholz (2001) notes the possibility that some people might be unable to benefit from a therapist's freer self-expression and self-disclosure because it might be experienced as frightening or intrusive. In the service of contributing to the discussion of therapist self-disclosure, we will illustrate its use in the case of the therapist's bearing witness to the other's traumatic experience.

Mary's therapist did not disclose her subjective experience of emotional distress during the beginning of their treatment out of concern that such disclosure would have compounded Mary's feelings of self-blame. Such disclosure might have added confirmation to Mary's organizing principle that she "could not do anything right" and that she had a hurtful effect on others.

Stern's research (1985) places the infant's initial development of a subjective self and the coinciding emergence of intersubjective relations between the seventh and ninth months of life. According to Stern, the essence of the subjective self is the infant's "momentous realization that inner subjective experiences . . . are potentially sharable with someone else" (p. 124). The infant's newfound recognition of mind, in self and other, makes it possible for the infant to interact with his caretakers in verbal and nonverbal communication. At this developmental moment, the infant establishes both subjectivity and the recognition of his or her own mind and inner experience and intersubjectivity or the sense that the other also has inner experiences. There is, then, the appreciation that communication or sharing between separate minds is possible.

Stern's work (1985) emphasizes the importance of a child's achievement of intersubjective relatedness because it recognizes that "an empathic process bridging the two minds has been created" (pp. 125–26). Out of this develops a capacity for a shared knowing among the dyad. This empathic connection between mother and child can be generalized to the dynamics between the participants in therapy.

As Mary's assault narrative unfolded in the intersubjective field, she revealed more details of the assault. She described her attacker's appearance—his long hair, the tattoo on his arm, his large stature. Following her disclosure about the assault outside of the bar, her therapist also became more vigilant when visiting the downtown area at night. Even when surrounded by friends who had no idea of her vigilance, the therapist's sense of vulnerability and disgust with the perpetrator were amplified. It helped the therapist appreciate that Mary's friends, too, had no idea of her level of emotional distress. In fact, like Mary, the therapist found herself avoiding the streets where Mary had been violently attacked. It became apparent that there was an experience of heightened intersubjective conjunction between the therapist and Mary.

Toward the end of treatment, reflecting on their work together, the therapist carefully determined to selectively disclose to Mary her own emotional distress in reaction to bearing witness to Mary's traumatic experience. The therapist shared with Mary her own hypervigilance when downtown and her acute awareness of men who might resemble the perpetrator's description. She shared with Mary how she, too, was drawn to watching crime stories on television, similar to what Mary had described. The therapist hoped that such self-disclosure would provide a reparative selfobject experience for Mary in the form of confirming the therapist as a witness to Mary's traumatic experience and affect states.

Such self-disclosure goes beyond articulating affect attunement such as, "It sounds like you were very frightened" or expressing sympathy by such statements as, "I would have been frightened and upset, too, if that happened to me." Rather, by sharing that "I feel frightened, too, when I walk downtown," the therapist is concretizing her witnessing function. Through the shared experience of fear and vulnerability, the therapist is conveying that she is there with Mary and together they have been emotionally affected by the assault. It depathologizes the experience of victimization, giving legitimacy and validity to the affective experience that neither empathy nor sympathy can fully convey.

There were three aspects to the therapist's self-disclosure that we believe were therapeutic for Mary. First, by bearing witness to Mary's trauma, the therapist's capacity to accept and tolerate Mary's disorganizing affective experience provided an important selfobject function. Correspondingly, Mary's reciprocal bearing of witness to her therapist's distress provided "interactive regulation" (Beebe and Lachmann 2002) for the pair. Secondly, Mary's capacity to regulate, modulate, and integrate disturbing affects was enhanced by the affirming, mirroring, and twinship selfobject experience with the therapist that mutual witnessing provided. Here we have self-disclosure as a selfobject function promoting the recognition, modulation, regulation, and integration of overwhelming affective experience. Thirdly, the therapist's self-disclosure of her own emotional upset could promote the depathologizing of Mary's overwhelming affective experience. Depathologizing Mary's trauma experience promoted self-delineation and self-cohesion. The therapist's self-disclosure of the effect Mary's traumatic experience had on her was therapeutic because of the "shared knowing" (Tosone et al. 2003) that it created.

After the disclosure, both participants could appreciate a kind of "reciprocal knowing" or "mutual recognition" wherein the powerful affects were experienced by both. The subtext of the therapist's self-disclosure conveyed to Mary, "You are not alone. I have been personally affected by your experience in a deep way. This relationship is real and is not confined to the therapy room." Most importantly, the disclosure communicated, "You matter." This served to disconfirm both Mary's mother's and attacker's messages of "you don't matter," and it established the conditions for new organizations of experience to take form.

Mary began to develop a greater sense of personal agency. She seemed to feel she had more control over her life. She felt less like a helpless victim and at that point determined to report the crime, despite her awareness that a prosecution would probably not follow. Correspondingly, Mary's therapist also felt less powerless and insecure professionally, as she began to feel a sense of mastery. At the outset of the treatment, Mary organized her experience in a way that seamlessly fit in with her feeling of being disposable, unimportant, inadequate, and hopeless. The therapist, too, organized her experience in a self-depreciating manner. She felt incapable, helpless, and incompetent. Their organizations of experience reflected one another, in that they confirmed similar feelings of self-blame and helplessness.

Although Mary was aware of the slim chances that any justice or retribution would occur, pressing charges would be symbolic of the change in her experience. Mary began to feel empowered in a way that was reorganizing and transforming. The assault was not something she deserved and it did not reflect any inadequacy or weakness. Her flashbacks decreased, her sleep improved, her depressive symptoms were reduced. She appeared less vulnerable, helpless, and fearful.

Mary's therapist's experience paralleled hers. The therapist, too, had felt less helpless, inadequate, and incompetent. Now, she felt empowered both personally and professionally, as a sense of mastery over the disturbing affects began to occur. Through the validation of Mary that was prompted by her therapist's self-disclosure, the therapist began to feel validated by Mary's witnessing of her therapist's distress. The therapist came to appreciate that her insecurity and experience of helplessness and incompetence was consistent with her inexperience as a therapist and did not reflect an inadequacy on her part. Rather, it reflected a typical response that is commonly experienced in a new professional.

At termination, Mary gave her therapist a letter. Mary's letter revealed her subjective experience of their work together. Mary described her new experience of feeling worthwhile and took newfound pride her ability to challenge the "voice" in her mind that says, "You aren't worth it. You are disposable, unimportant, and invisible." This "voice" was her previous organization of experience. Mary had successfully acknowledged and honored her affect surrounding the event and altered it to fit her new organization of experience that she was worthwhile. The "voice" still existed, but the message of old organizing principles had receded into the background.

Were Mary's changes responsible for her therapist's changes or were her therapist's changes responsible for Mary's? We propose that, as intersubjective systems theory suggests, the changes were co-constructed by two subjectivities coming together. What was traumatizing for Mary was the meaning she had made of her subjective experience that the brutal assault was deserved; a reflection of her organizing principle that she was inadequate and unimportant. She believed that she should have been able to prevent it, fight it, avoid it. Others were not victimized—she was. The therapist's bearing witness, self-disclosure, validation, and attunement to Mary's subjective experience challenged this organizing principle. In the therapeutic relationship, Mary was visible, important, and valuable. The therapist's subjective experience of Mary's assault was that Mary was a victim of a violent intrusion that was in no way was invited or deserved. Mary's awareness of and bearing witness to her therapist's subjective experience following the self-disclosure challenged the therapist's own subjective experience of helplessness and vulnerability.

Although her therapist's self-disclosure was helpful in disconfirming Mary's prior organization of experience and promoted new ways of organizing her experience, we are not recommending that this be seen as a technique for helping traumatized people in general. Such self-disclosure had a positive impact on the intersubjective field Mary and her therapist created. It was helpful for the two of them. However, that it was helpful for the two of them in no way assures that it would be helpful for any other therapy dyad. We think that this therapist's self-disclosure served important witnessing, mirroring, twinship, and self-delineating selfobject functions for Mary, and reciprocally for the therapist. Similar conditions might arise in other therapeutic relationships that would allow therapist witnessing and self-disclosure to serve selfobject functions for the other. While self-disclosure turned out to also serve the mirroring and twinship needs of the therapist, the important assessment to be made is whether some action of the therapist will serve the best interests of the other. This can be hard to predict in advance; but the attuned therapist can be vigilant to the impact that her or his actions might have on the other and respond accordingly.

Chapter Eight

The Wolf Man's Subjective Experience of His Treatment with Freud

Coauthored with Pamela Haglund, PsyD

Little is known about how Freud conducted a treatment. There are, of course, his technical papers and recommendations, but these seem to have been written more to protect people from the wild analyses conducted by physicians who learned about psychoanalysis from reading Freud's writings than as reflections of Freud's actual technique. Even Freud's few case studies disappoint in this area. They were written to illustrate the validity of Freud's theoretical formulations rather than as models of how a psychoanalysis ought to be conducted.

Because Freud never described his actual technique, the only source of information about how he worked comes from the recollections of his analysands. A number of his analysands, primarily students seeking to become trained in or knowledgeable about psychoanalysis, kept diaries of their experiences in consulting with Freud (e.g., Blanton 1971; Wortis 1954). But of all the people Freud treated, we know the most about one of the most famous: Serge Pankejeff, the Wolf Man.

In addition to Freud's (1955b [1918]) extensive case report and some subsequent comments (1964 [1937]), we also have Pankejeff's own memoirs (Pankejeff 1971a), as well as his recollections of his treatment with Freud (Pankejeff 1971b). Brunswick, to whom Freud referred Pankejeff for further analysis, has also published her discussion of the treatment (Brunswick 1971 [1928]), and Gardiner (1971) has contributed her recollections of him in his later life. Lubin (1967) has also published excerpts of an interview with Pankejeff focusing on his religious upbringing. And finally, there is a remarkable series of interviews, conducted by a German journalist (Obholzer 1982), that Pankejeff gave toward the end of his life. This rich record, particularly Pankejeff's own recollections, provides a unique window into Freud's consulting room. Apparently, there exists in the Freud archives a wealth of letters and interview materials collected by Eissler that regrettably have not been made public yet.

Pankejeff's recollections form not a record of how Freud worked but a portrait of Pankejeff's subjective experience of his encounter with Freud. As Magid (1993) pointed out, "just as we grant a subjective validity to a patient's account of his parents many years after the fact, so we must grant to Serge's later memoirs the subjective validity of what he himself came to see as most important in his own story and treatment" (p. 158).

As we review Freud's report of the Wolf Man case, as well as Pankejeff's recollections of his subjective experience of Freud and the treatment, a picture of Freud's technique emerges that is at variance, if not at odds, with what Lipton (1977) referred to as "modern psychoanalytic technique." As we shall try to illustrate in what follows, Freud was selective in what he identified as his psychoanalytic technique, omitting a discussion of those interventions Pankejeff found most meaningful in his treatment. On the one hand, Freud appears to have responded to Pankejeff's longings for experiences of idealization and mirroring by creating a context in which these selfobject needs would be provided. This aspect of the treatment appears to be quite compatible with the technical recommendations of self psychology. On the other hand, by adhering to the principles of drive theory and the concomitant technical stance of promoting regression, analyzing resistance, and reconstructing the infantile neurosis, Freud created a context of intersubjective disjunction. According to Stolorow and Atwood (1992), "Disjunction . . . occurs when the therapist assimilates the material expressed by the patient into configurations that significantly alter its meaning for the patient" (p. 103). The intersubjective disjunction in this treatment refers to Freud's insistence on imposing his own theoretical formulations on Pankejeff's childhood experience, rather than understanding the subjective meaning of the experience for Pankejeff. As we will develop later, Freud's agenda for this treatment was to use the Pankejeff case to confirm his conviction about the centrality of infantile sexuality in personality development. By imposing his agenda onto Pankejeff's subjective experience, Freud contributed to Pankejeff's attitude of obliging apathy, which he misunderstood as resistance to treatment.

From the perspective of Pankejeff's subjective experience of Freud, we will argue that Freud was engaging in an inconsistent and incomplete analysis of the selfobject and repetitive dimensions of the transferences (Stolorow and Atwood 1992). Whether intentionally or inadvertently, Freud did occasionally respond to the archaic selfobject longings of Pankejeff by providing opportunities for the development and unfolding of idealizing and mirroring transferences. Regrettably for Pankejeff, Freud neglected to maintain a consistent stance regarding Pankejeff's archaic selfobject longings. Freud failed to understand the way Pankejeff's early experience had become organized and how his relationship with Freud was filtered through this organization of experience. In fact, through the application of Freud's more classical technique, he subjected Pankejeff to experiences of affective misattunement that were narcissistically injurious and then missed important opportunities for repair. Nevertheless, what remain impressive are the gains, however transitory, that Pankejeff made as a result of his relationship with Freud. Unfortunately, these gains appear fragile in the face of Freud's misattunements and those of Pankejeff's second analyst, Ruth Mack Brunswick.

What we have identified as Freud's intuitive self psychological technique (the provision of idealizing and mirroring selfobject functions through empathic listening and affect attunement) have typically been viewed as either Freud's errors of technique or as benign, but therapeutically inert interventions (Lipton 1977). Langs (1972) has thoroughly catalogued "the multitude of deviations and extensions of the boundaries of the patient-analyst relationship" (p. 377) under the general heading of "the misalliance dimension" of Freud's relationship with the Wolf Man. These misalliances involved Freud's famous parameter (Eissler 1953) of setting and sticking to a forced termination date; treating Pankejeff for free; raising money for Pankejeff's support; explaining and educating Pankejeff about Freud's theories; giving explicit advice to Pankejeff on how to live his life; sharing personal anecdotes and confidences with Pankejeff; and making indiscreet remarks about others he treated, as well as about professional colleagues. According to Langs (1972), "This myriad of misalliances and transference gratifications went unrecognized, uncorrected, and unanalyzed by Freud; their repercussions and their influence on the Wolf Man's psychopathology and fantasy life went unmodified" (p. 377).

A somewhat more benevolent spin was put on Freud's conduct by Lipton (1977). Lipton's position (which focused on the Rat Man case but may also be applied to the Wolf Man case) is that much of what Langs would call the "misalliance dimension" of Freud's clinical work could be differently understood as aspects of the "unobjectionable positive transference," characteristics of interpersonal relations that involve tact and courtesy rather than agents of therapeutic technique. As examples of the unobjectionable positive transference, Freud's deviations of technique and boundary extensions can be viewed as, at best, benign interventions, doing no harm to the ongoing treatment, or, at worst, as inert reagents, having no discernible impact on the chemistry of the analytic relationship. In either case, Langs's worst-case scenario of Freud's misalliance dimension or Lipton's more benevolent view of Freud's interventions as harmless or unobjectionable, there is no recognition that it is specifically in this arena that Pankejeff experienced Freud's treatment as beneficial.

We will attempt to demonstrate in the rest of this chapter that what Langs criticized as Freud's misalliance dimension and Lipton defended as unobjectionable and harmless are, from the perspective of a self psychologically informed intersubjective systems theory, important aspects of the treatment relationship that Pankejeff experienced as therapeutic. We suggest that Pankejeff's gains in treatment derived largely from the self–selfobject relationship with Freud, and the transitory and unstable history of these improvements resulted from Freud's erratic and inconsistent attention to the selfobject and repetitive dimensions of the treatment and the resulting intersubjective disjunctions. Because Freud did not appreciate or understand the therapeutic impact of the selfobject dimension of the treatment, he did not focus on its illumination or transformation. It is only when we turn to Pankejeff's subjective experience of his treatment with Freud that we see the importance of the selfobject dimension of the relationship with Freud for the repair of Pankejeff's damaged self-organization.

SERGE PANKEJEFF'S HISTORY

In 1910, Serge Pankejeff, at the age of twenty-four, was brought to Freud for treatment by his physician after suffering from intractable depression for several years. Pankejeff was the second child and only son of a wealthy Russian aristocrat whose parents traveled frequently for long periods of time throughout his childhood. In their absence, the children were left in the care of nursemaids, tutors, and servants. Pankejeff's primary caregiver was Nanya, a peasant woman who had lost her own son and in whose room the boy slept until age seven or eight years old. Pankejeff's only sibling was a sister two years older, who committed suicide when he was nineteen years old. Their father favored the highly intelligent and precocious daughter. Pankejeff experienced his mother as cool, undemonstrative, and lacking tenderness (Obholzer 1982, p. 74). She apparently suffered abdominal problems and was somewhat hypochondriacal during the boy's childhood. Pankejeff recalled that she was particularly attentive to him when he was ill.

Pankejeff's father and several uncles appear to have suffered from serious mental illnesses, and at least three close relatives committed suicide. From the time the boy was five years old, his father made extensive stays at sanitoria for the treatment of manic-depressive symptoms. At least one uncle, a favorite of Pankejeff's, became schizophrenic, apparently chronically paranoid. His sister displayed depressive and schizophrenic symptoms.

Freud's initial analytic work with Pankejeff lasted four years. Following a five-year interval that coincided with World War I, he had a brief second analysis of less than one year with Freud. Pankejeff repeatedly sought treatment throughout the remainder of his life. During the first analysis, Freud focused on the earliest behavioral problems reported by Pankejeff—a period of aggressiveness at age four, then animal phobias and sadistic and masochistic wishes, followed by obsessions with religious and sacrilegious themes. What Freud believed ultimately held the secret to Pankejeff's pathology, and the basis of the term "Wolf Man," was a childhood dream:

> I dreamt that it was night and that I was lying in my bed. My bed stood with its foot towards the window; in front of the window there was a row of old walnut trees. I know it was winter when I had the dream, and nighttime. Suddenly the window opened of its own accord, and I was terrified to see that some white wolves were sitting on the big walnut tree in front of the window. There were six or seven of them. The wolves were quite white, and looked more like foxes or sheep-dogs, for they had big tails like foxes and they had their ears pricked like dogs when they pay attention to something. In greater terror, evidently of being eaten up by the wolves, I screamed (and woke up) (Freud 1955b [1918], p. 29).

Based on this dream, Freud reconstructed what he considered to be the kernel of Pankejeff's childhood neurosis—viewing the primal scene at age eighteen months. Pankejeff's unresolved difficulties stemming from reactions to this initial trauma were seen as the foundation of all subsequent symptomatology. In Freud's view, these problems included a passive homosexual orientation based on identification with his mother, a wish to be related to the father in a way comparable to her, and fears of castration by his father.

SERGE PANKEJEFF'S SELFOBJECT NEEDS

Others have discussed in detail Pankejeff's diagnostic presentation (Blum 1972; Brunswick 1971 [1928]; Langs 1972; Magid 1993, Meissner 1977; Thomas 1992). The consensus opinion is that Pankejeff is an example of a narcissistic personality disorder. Specifically, Pankejeff manifested in both his variety of symptoms and in his transferences to Freud and to Brunswick unmet developmental needs for mirroring and for an idealized selfobject. Furthermore, Pankejeff appears to us to have presented consistently over his lifetime with the kind of depletion depression that we now understand to be a variation of narcissistic disturbance (Brandchaft 1988; Lachmann and Beebe 1996; Palombo 1985; Stolorow, Brandchaft, and Atwood 1987).

Development of a healthy, resilient sense of self depends on the consistent availability of selfobjects during infancy and early childhood (Beebe and Lachmann 1992; Kohut 1971, 1977). By affectively attuned attention to the needs of the child, including those for enthusiastic affirmation of the child's grandiosity and sensitive matching and regulation of affect states, caregivers (and other significant persons) contribute to the formation of a stable, cohesive, and positively colored sense of self.

Palombo (1985) described the experience of depression from a self psychological perspective. He stated that depression "is best understood as reflective of a depletion of the self . . . resulting from an irreconcilable yearning within the self for a missing selfobject function" (p. 33). In other words, something is missing within the self, and the narcissistically depressed individual seeks revitalization through relationships or activities that provide the unavailable selfobject function.

Freud (1955 [1918]) discussed Pankejeff in terms of childhood obsessions and phobias that arose ultimately as a consequence of viewing the primal scene at eighteen months. However, the conditions for which Pankejeff sought treatment from Freud in 1910 were recurrent depressions spanning the previous five years. In Pankejeff's words,

> [M]y annihilating remorse had reduced me to such a state of profound depression that I was incapable of coming to any decision or entering upon any activity whatsoever. The very worst, however, was that since all my efforts to be cured had failed so deplorably, I now considered my condition absolutely hopeless. There was no way out (Pankejeff 1971a, p. 79).

During those years prior to entering treatment with Freud, Pankejeff recalled becoming psychologically ill after he contracted gonorrhea at age seventeen (Obholzer 1982, p. 28). Although he reported few details of his illness, he described traveling with his mother and sister as a diversion for what was diagnosed as a "puberty neurosis." Within the next four years he experienced significant turmoil, loss, and depression. In 1906, his sister Anna, his closest childhood companion, committed suicide by poisoning herself with mercury; his father died suddenly in the summer of 1908 at age forty-nine from what Pankejeff speculated was an overdose of sleeping medication; and his Uncle Peter, whom he "had loved . . . better than any of my other uncles or aunts or even my parents" (Pankejeff 1971a, p. 80), died in 1909. Pankejeff visited many sanitoria and traveled extensively during this period in attempts to overcome the "'lack of relationships' and spiritual vacuum in which life was 'empty, everything seemed unreal'" (Pankejeff 1971a, p. 50).

In the midst of these losses, during a stay at a sanitarium near Munich, Pankejeff fell in love with Therese (winter, 1908). They began a tumultuous relationship in which both alternatively committed to a future together and withdrew from the commitment. Pankejeff's doctors and his mother opposed the relationship on grounds that she was beneath his level socially and that he was not stable enough to make a decision to marry her. It was in this emotional state that Pankejeff met Freud in January 1910 and entered into an analysis with him.

We suggest that Pankejeff was experiencing a depression based in part on the loss of the tie to those family members who held the promise of providing the sustaining selfobject functions he desperately needed. In each case, the needed soothing, idealizing, and affirming functions provided by these loved ones were inconsistent and ultimately inadequate. That is, these object ties did not support Pankejeff's acquisition of sustained self-regulatory capacities. Furthermore, these early object relationships were not ones in which overwhelming affects could be integrated and ruptured selfobject connections repaired. For example, his relationship with his sister was contaminated by incestuous experiences that he believed were never adequately resolved. He claimed that "the sister complex" and its effect "ruined his life" (Obholzer 1982, p. 37). Further, his father was one whom Pankejeff admired and wished to please. However, during childhood his father preferred Anna. After Anna's death, Pankejeff attempted a "rapprochement" with his father, but the effort failed due to the "devastating influence of [Pankejeff's] ambivalence" (Pankejeff 1971a, p. 38).

Perhaps as important as his unresolved grief over the death of important people in his life is the evidence of his emotional isolation and abandonment during his childhood. Though he lived a privileged life, Pankejeff's recollections suggest that neither his mother nor his father functioned as available, attuned selfobjects, responsive to his emotional needs or affective experience. Furthermore, because his relationship with his mother was so inconsistent and distant, and she herself was likely to have been grief stricken by the loss of her daughter and husband, it is unlikely that she would have been available to provide an attuned response to his grief over these losses.

Therefore, when Serge Pankejeff met Freud, his inner resources were depleted. The deficiency of his inner resources derived from his chronic experiences of loss and accompanying affective misattunements, the repair of which could no longer be salvaged in real life. At that point, Pankejeff reported that his connection to Therese was the only attachment that sustained and affirmed him.

SERGE PANKEJEFF'S SELFOBJECT TRANSFERENCES

Prior to entering treatment with Freud, Pankejeff had consulted many of the most eminent psychiatrists and neurologists of his time, to no avail.

Apparently, the aspect of being connected to an eminent practitioner, the action of an idealizing transference, was not sufficient to produce even a "transference cure." To appreciate why the connection to an eminently idealizable practitioner produced no improvement in Pankejeff's condition, we should turn to his subjective experience, as expressed in his own words:

> The neurotic went to a physician with the wish to pour out his heart to him, and was bitterly disappointed when the physician would scarcely listen to the problems which so troubled him, much less try to understand them. But that which to the doctor was only an unimportant by-product of a serious objective condition was for the neurotic himself a profound inner experience. So there could be no real contact between patient and physician (Pankejeff 1971b, pp. 135–36).

With Freud, Pankejeff had a different experience. "Freud's whole attitude, and the way in which he listened to me, differentiated him strikingly from his famous colleagues whom I had hitherto known and in whom I had found such a lack of deeper psychological understanding" (Pankejeff 1971b, p. 137). In terms of the subjective experiences of affect attunement and feeling understood, Pankejeff said (1971b), "It will be easy to imagine the sense of relief I now felt when Freud asked me various questions about my childhood and about the relationships in my family, and listened with the greatest attention to all I had to say. Occasionally he let fall some remark which bore witness to his complete understanding of everything I had experienced" (p. 138).

Pankejeff described other characteristics of his experiences with Freud that made this a unique therapeutic relationship. First, "Freud's appearance was such as to win my confidence immediately . . . the most impressive feature was his intelligent dark eyes, which looked at me penetratingly but without causing me the slightest feeling of discomfort" (Pankejeff 1971b, p. 137).

Second, it was "a revelation" (Pankejeff 1971b, p. 138) for Pankejeff to hear the fundamental concepts of psychoanalysis, the new science, "from the mouth of its founder" (p. 138). As we learn later in Pankejeff's recollections, Freud was eager to teach him about psychoanalysis, both the metapsychology and the theory of technique. Pankejeff went on to report that he was flattered by Freud's viewing him as a bright and perceptive student of psychoanalysis. In addition, Freud was with Pankejeff, as with many of his other analysands, indiscreet about those he was treating and his professional colleagues, as well as self-disclosing his own personal life. These communications clearly contributed to Pankejeff's feeling of specialness.

Third, Pankejeff experienced Freud as mirroring, affirming, and validating of his relationship with Therese, the most important person in his current life. In his experience with other psychiatrists, Pankejeff's relationship with Therese was viewed as a manifestation of his neurosis, and it was recommended that he give her up. But, as Freud reassured him, "the 'breakthrough to the woman' could under certain circumstances be considered the neurotic's greatest achievement, a sign of his will to live, an active attempt to recover" (Pankejeff 1971b, p. 138). According to Pankejeff's subjective experience of Freud's technique, Pankejeff concluded that Freud "attempted always to support and strengthen the kernel of health, separated from the chaff of neurosis" (Pankejeff 1971b, p. 138).

These, then, were some of the important actions of Freud that facilitated Pankejeff's development of idealizing and mirroring selfobject transferences. Clearly, Freud's disclosures and indiscretions, while at odds with his own technical recommendations (Freud 1958b [1912], 1958a [1913], 1958c [1914]), provided new experiences of being valued and understood that enhanced Pankejeff's vulnerable self-organization. However, our emphasis is on the meaning these disclosures and indiscretions had for Pankejeff.

Pankejeff's comments attest to his yearning for experiences of affirmation, specialness, and attunement from an idealized selfobject. However, Freud's theory did not include these formulations. He believed that Pankejeff's problems derived from conflicted infantile psychosexual development. He considered that Pankejeff's primarily passive transference (obliging apathy) derived from his latent homosexuality and unresolved love for his father and identification with his mother. Out of this understanding, Freud chose to confront Pankejeff's ambivalence, which he believed stemmed from repressed infantile sexual experiences. After approximately three years of analysis, Freud arbitrarily set a termination date for one year hence, the summer of 1914.

This move by Freud to end the analysis represents another intersubjective disjunction in the treatment. Freud (1964 [1937]) clearly felt frustrated and disappointed with Pankejeff's progress and to avoid the treatment failing, he "resorted to the heroic measure of fixing a time-limit for the analysis" (p. 217). By assimilating Pankejeff's apparent lack of motivation to continue changing into his theory of resistance, Freud failed to understand the meaning the treatment had for Pankejeff. Freud did not appreciate that a developmental process had been set in motion in the analysis in which he was experienced by Pankejeff as the attuned, understanding presence that Pankejeff had never adequately had available to him. In his misattuned alliance with Pankejeff, Freud ultimately reflected back to the young man what was in Freud's mind's eye, not what was presented to him. Freud theorized that Pankejeff's early childhood obsessions and phobias were inadequately resolved and that they and the later depressions derived from repression of the memory of the primal scene.

What Pankejeff required and what Freud partially and inconsistently provided was the opportunity to reengage a thwarted developmental process. In the mirroring transference with Freud, Pankejeff experienced restored self-object functions of affirmation and affect attunement. In his discussions with Obholzer almost sixty years after the analysis with Freud, Pankejeff recalled his life in Vienna at the time: "When Freud treated me, I was fine. I felt very good. We went out, to the cafes, to the Prater, it was a pleasant life" (Obholzer 1982, p. 39).

We speculate that if Freud had operated from a contextual understanding of the meaning of the treatment relationship to Pankejeff, had understood the developmental imperative for Pankejeff to experience both affirmation and attunement with him as an idealized and mirroring selfobject, had noticed and responded to the ruptures in the self-selfobject bond, had articulated the fear of retraumatization that characterized the repetitive dimension of the transference, and had examined his countertransferential needs to use Pankejeff's case to confirm his theories, the gains made by Pankejeff might have been sustained after the treatment ended. Much of what Freud did and how he related to Pankejeff actually met his selfobject needs. However, because Freud believed that psychological change derived from recalling and interpreting infantile sexual and aggressive conflicts, he missed the opportunity for a more enduring outcome.

SERGE PANKEJEFF'S INCOMPLETE CURE

Ironically, Pankejeff expressed exactly these sentiments in his interviews with Obholzer. "Knowledge and memory, knowledge and interpretation, aren't enough. There must be some additional experience. And that experience didn't occur" (Obholzer 1982, p. 110). This comment was made in response to the revelation to Pankejeff by Obholzer that she, like he, once had gonorrhea. Pankejeff went on to say that he believed that if he were younger, a cure might come from the freedom he felt with her disclosure. We consider this an example of a moment of affect attunement, a shared recognition that contributes to a more stable self-organization by validating one's subjective experience. The selfobject function of this type of self-disclosure is consistent with the discussion in chapter 7. It represents a kind of affective matching that contributes to vitality and positive well-being. These experiences occur frequently, no doubt, in psychological treatments based on a variety of theories. Only recently have we begun to appreciate the central role they play in psychological change.

What was not addressed in Freud's therapeutic efforts were Pankejeff's experiences of disappointment and grief over the lost or failed selfobject relationships of his childhood. In Freud's summary of the chronology of the events mentioned in the case history, he omitted listing any of the losses Pankejeff suffered (Freud 1955b [1918], p. 121). Freud's neglect of the importance of grief in Pankejeff's case is all the more striking when we consider that Freud's seminal paper on mourning and melancholia was published just the previous year, in 1917. Instead of focusing on Pankejeff's grief, Freud, consistently interpreted Pankejeff's symptoms as resulting from his latent homosexual longings for his father.

From an intersubjective systems perspective, Freud's need for Pankejeff to confirm his theories, essentially Freud's need to be mirrored by Pankejeff, contaminated the treatment. Freud approached the treatment looking to find confirmation for his theory of infantile sexuality. He wanted clinical material that would refute the claims of Adler and Jung and he wrote the Wolf Man case for this purpose. Offenkrantz and Tobin (1973) reported that as early as the autumn of 1912, Freud, in a request published in *Zentralblatt für Psychoanalyse*, sought dream material that "justifies the conclusion that the dreamers have been witnesses of sexual intercourse in their early years" (Freud 1912, p. 680). Showing some awareness of Freud's ulterior motive, Pankejeff commented to Obholzer (1982), regarding the forced termination, that "I always talked about something. But he didn't find what he was after, whatever it was" (p. 40). Unfortunately, Freud's needs to be mirrored and to have his theories validated were not compatible with Pankejeff's needs to be mirrored and to have his own subjective experience attuned to. Freud, by seeing Pankejeff as passive and resistant, was replicating Pankejeff's experiences with his disinterested father. By misinterpreting Pankejeff's dynamics to fit the theory of infantile sexuality, Freud missed the opportunity to repair the experience of hurt and rejection that accompanied Pankejeff's father's preference for the more precocious sister.

Freud complained (Gardiner 1971) that "the patient . . . remained for a long time entrenched in an attitude of obliging apathy. He listened, understood, and remained unapproachable" (p. 157). Our understanding of Pankejeff's behavior is that this stance reflects the repetitive dimension of the transference: that Pankejeff was attempting to preserve his connection with the idealized and needed Freud while at the same time seeking to avoid experiences of retraumatization. It further illustrates what Brandchaft (1994) has referred to as "pathological structures of accommodation." In the case of Pankejeff, this sheds different light on what Freud observed as Pankejeff's resistance to changing. Pankejeff's need to accommodate himself to his perception of the needs or wishes of the other, at the cost of being true to himself, was a prominent feature of his relationship with both Freud and Brunswick as well as other psychoanalytic emissaries, like Lubin.

Lubin (1967) developed the hypothesis that the drawing of the tree with the wolves sitting on the branches derived from Pankejeff's memory of the shape of the Russian Orthodox cross. Lubin very much wanted Pankejeff to read and comment on (approve of) his manuscript and he went through the effort of having it translated into German. He reported that he saw Pankejeff again, after he had studied the manuscript. According to Lubin's report, "He [Pankejeff] brimmed with enthusiasm, declared that my hypothesis was probably correct, and failed to criticize a single point in the manuscript. I became skeptical about this praise when I found he was more reluctant than on the previous visit to probe his memories about religion" (Lubin 1967, p. 160).

In connection with Pankejeff's accommodating to his impression of Freud's expectations for him, there is an important letter and commentary by Pankejeff that has been published (Pankejeff 1957). Pankejeff's letter, dated June 6, 1926, is in reply to a letter from Freud, who posed several questions about the Wolf-dream. In his commentary, Pankejeff said, "As my letter to him shows, the chief question was whether I had seen the opera *Pique Dame* before the Wolf-dream. I am at present still of the opinion that I saw *Pique Dame* after the dream" (p. 458). Later Pankejeff adds, "Now it would suit the interpretation of the Wolf-dream much better if the contrary were the case and if I had been to the opera before I had my dream. Unfortunately all of my memories speak against this" (p. 458). In both instances, Lubin's hypothesis and Freud's query about the Pique Dame opera, Pankejeff demonstrated his eagerness to accommodate to what he perceived as the expectations of Freud and other analysts.

Pankejeff's depression, "obliging apathy," and accommodation obscured his intense longing for someone who would appreciate his "innermost self" (Brandchaft 1988). As long as the transference was understood as a repetition of the wish for a homosexual relationship with his father in which Pankejeff would take the passive role, the best that Pankejeff could do was to "oblige" Freud. The stance prevented the loss of yet another selfobject, one that provided cohesion and harmony for Pankejeff's inadequate self-organization. However, had the transferences been understood as the reengagement of an essential developmental process, it is possible that Pankejeff would have been able to successfully integrate the disruptive affect states of grief and depression and the intense longing for affirmation, leading to the consolidation of a healthier self-organization.

Bibliography

Adler, E., and J. L. Bachant. 1998. *Working in depth*. Northvale, NJ: Jason Aronson.

Alarcon, R. D., E. F. Foulks, and M. Vakkur. 1998. *Personality disorders and culture*. New York: John Wiley & Sons.

Altman, N. 1995. *The analyst in the inner city: Race, class, and culture through a psychoanalytic lens*. Hillsdale, NJ: Analytic Press.

———. 2000. Black and white thinking: A psychoanalyst considers race. *Psychoanalytic Dialogues* 10:589–605.

American Psychiatric Association. 2000. *Diagnostic and statistical manual of mental disorders*. 4th ed., text revision. Washington, DC: The American Psychiatric Association.

———. 2002. Guidelines on multicultural education, training, research, practice, and organizational change for psychologists. http://www.apa.org/pi/ multiculturalguidelines/ diversity.html.

Arlow, J. A. 1994. Aggression and prejudice: Some psychoanalytic observations on the blood libel accusation against the Jews. In *The spectrum of psychoanalysis: Essays in honor of Martin S. Bergmann*, ed. A. K. Richards and A. D. Richards, 283–94. Madison, CT: International Universities Press.

Aron, L. 1996. *A meeting of minds*. Hillsdale, NJ: Analytic Press.

Atwood, G. E., and R. D. Stolorow. 1984. *Structures of subjectivity: Explorations in psychoanalytic phenomenology*. Hillsdale, NJ: Analytic Press.

———. 1997. Defects in the self: Liberating concept or imprisoning metaphor? *Psychoanalytic Dialogues* 7:517–22.

Auden, W. H. 1940. *Another time*. New York: Random House.

Beebe, B., and F. M. Lachmann. 1992. The contribution of mother-infant mutual influence to the origins of self and object representations. In *Relational perspectives in psychoanalysis*, ed. N. J. Skolnick and S. C. Warshaw, 83–117. Hillsdale, NJ: Analytic Press.

———. 2002. *Infant research and adult treatment: Co-constructing interactions*. Hillsdale, NJ: Analytic Press.

Benjamin, J. 1990. An outline of intersubjectivity: The development of recognition. *Psychoanalytic Psychology* 7:33–46.

———. 1995a. An outline of intersubjectivity: the development of recognition. *Psychoanalytic Psychology* 7 (Suppl.):33–46.

———. 1995b. *Like subjects, love objects: Essays on recognition and sexual difference.* New Haven, CT: Yale University Press.

Blanton, S. 1971. *Diary of my analysis with Sigmund Freud.* New York: Hawthorn Books.

Blum, H. P. 1972. The borderline childhood of the Wolf Man. In *Freud and his patients*, Vol. II, ed. M. Kanzer and J. Glenn, 341–57. New York: Aronson.

Brandchaft, B. 1988. A case of intractable depression. In *Learning from Kohut: Progress in self psychology*, ed. A. Goldberg. Hillsdale, NJ: Analytic Press.

———. 1994. To free the spirit from its cell. In *The intersubjective perspective*, ed. R. D. Stolorow, G. E. Atwood, and B. Brandchaft. Northvale, NJ: Jason Aronson.

Brandon, R., and C. Davies. 1973. *Wrongful imprisonment.* London: Allen & Unwin.

Brenner, C. 2002. Conflict, compromise formation, and structural theory. *Psychoanalytic Quarterly* 71:397–417.

Breuer, J., and S. Freud. 1955 [1893–1895]. *Studies on hysteria* (Standard edition, Vol. 11). London: Hogarth Press.

Brunswick, R. M. 1971 [1928]. A supplement to Freud's "History of an infantile neurosis." In *The Wolf-Man by the Wolf-Man*, ed. M. Gardiner. New York: Basic Books.

Bucci, W. 2002. The challenge of diversity in modern psychoanalysis. *Psychoanalytic Psychology* 19:216–26.

Buirski, P., and P. Haglund. 1999. The selfobject function of interpretation. *Progress in self psychology: Volume 15.* Hillsdale, NJ: Analytic Press.

———. 2001. *Making sense together: The intersubjective approach to psychotherapy.* Northvale, NJ: Jason Aronson.

Buirski, P., and M. Monroe. 2000. Intersubjective observations on transference love. *Psychoanalytic Psychology* 17:78–87.

Castillo, R. J. 1997. *Culture and mental illness: A client-centered approach.* Pacific Grove, CA: Brooks/Cole.

Cavell, M. 1993. *The psychoanalytic mind: From Freud to philosophy.* Cambridge, MA: Harvard University Press.

Chatham, P. M. 1996. *Treatment of the borderline personality disorder.* Northvale, NJ: Jason Aronson.

Cook, H., and P. Buirski. 1990. Countertransference in psychoanalytic supervision: An heuristic model. *Psychoanalysis and Psychotherapy* 8:77–87.

Crits-Christoph, P., E. Frank, D. L. Chambless, C. Brody, and J. F. Karp. 1995. Training in empirically validated treatments: What are clinical psychology students learning? *Professional Psychology: Research and Practice* 26:514–22.

D'Andrea, M. 2003. Expanding our understanding of white racism and resistance to change in the fields of counseling and psychology. In *Culturally diverse mental health: The challenges of research and resistance*, ed. J. S. Mio and G. Y. Iwamasa. New York: Brunner-Routledge.

Danieli, Y. 1985. The treatment and prevention of long-term effects and intergenerational transmission of victimization: A lesson from Holocaust survivors and their children. In *Trauma and its wake*, Vol. 1, ed. C. R. Figley, 295–313. New York: Brunner/Mazel.

Eissler, K. R. 1953. The effect of the structure of the ego on psychoanalytic technique. *Journal of the American Psychoanalytic Association* 1:104–43.

Ellison, K., and R. Buckhout. 1981. *Psychology and criminal justice*. New York: Harper & Row.

Farmer, P. 2003. *Pathologies of power*. Berkeley: University of California Press.

Follette, V. M., M. M. Polusny, and K. Milbeck. 1994. Mental health and law enforcement professionals: Trauma history, psychological symptoms, and impact of providing services to child sexual abuse survivors. *Professional Psychology: Research and Practice* 25:275–82.

Freud, S. 1912. Request for example of childhood dreams. *Zentralblatt für Psychoanalyse* 2:680.

———. 1953 [1905a]. *Fragment of an analysis of a case of hysteria* (Standard edition, Vol. VII). London: Hogarth Press.

———. 1953 [1905b]. *Three essays on a theory of sexuality* (Standard edition, Vol. VII) London: Hogarth Press.

———. 1955a [1920]. Beyond the pleasure principle. In *Standard edition of the complete psychological works of Sigmund Freud XVIII*, ed. and trans. J. Strachey. London: Hogarth Press.

———. 1955b [1918]. From the history of an infantile neurosis. In *Standard edition of the complete psychological works of Sigmund Freud XVII*, ed. and trans. J. Strachey, 3–122. London: Hogarth Press.

———. 1958a [1913]. On beginning the treatment (further recommendations on the technique of psycho-analysis I). In *Standard edition of the complete psychological works of Sigmund Freud XII*, ed. and trans. J. Strachey, 12–144. London: Hogarth Press.

———. 1958b [1912]. Recommendations to physicians practicing psycho-analysis. In *Standard edition of the complete psychological works of Sigmund Freud XII*, ed. and trans. J. Strachey, 111–20. London: Hogarth Press.

———. 1958c [1914]. Remembering, repeating and working through (further recommendations on the technique of psycho-analysis II). In *Standard edition of the complete psychological works of Sigmund Freud XII*, ed. and trans. J. Strachey, 147–56. London: Hogarth Press.

———. 1961 [1923]. The ego and the id. In *Standard edition of the complete psychological works of Sigmund Freud XIX*, ed. and trans. J. Strachey, 12–67. London: Hogarth Press.

———. 1964 [1937]. Analysis terminable and interminable. In *Standard edition of the complete psychological works of Sigmund Freud XXIII*, ed. and trans. J. Strachey, 209–53. London: Hogarth Press.

Gadamer, H. 1975/1991. *Truth and method*. New York: Crossroads.

Gardiner, M. 1971. The Wolf-Man in later life. In *The Wolf-Man by the Wolf-Man*, ed. M. Gardiner. New York: Basic Books.

Gay, P. 1989. *The Freud reader*. New York: W.W. Norton.

Genest M., J. Levine, V. Ramsden, and R. Swanson. 1990. The impact of providing help: Emergency workers and cardiopulmary resuscitation attempts. *Journal of Traumatic Stress* 3:305–13.

Gilbert, M. C., and K. Evans. 2000. *Psychotherapy supervision: An integrative relational approach to psychotherapy supervision*. Philadelphia: Open University Press.

Gill, M. 1976. Metapsychology is not psychology. In *Psychology versus metapsychology: Psychoanalytic essays in memory of George S. Klein*, ed. M. Gill and P. Holzman. New York: International Universities Press.

Gobodo-Madikizela, P. 2003. *A human being died that night: A South African story of forgiveness*. Boston: Houghton Mifflin.

Goldner, V. 2004. When love hurts. *Psychoanalytic Inquiry* 24:346–72.

Goldstein, E. G. 1994. Self-disclosure in treatment: What therapists do and don't talk about. *Journal of Clinical Social Work* 22:417–33.

Goodman, D. J. 2001. *Promoting diversity and social justice: Educating people from privileged groups*. Thousand Oaks, CA: Sage.

Goretti, G. R. 2001. The myth and history of some psychoanalytic concepts. *International Journal of Psychoanalysis* 82:1205–23.

Greenberg, J. R., and S. A. Mitchell. 1983. *Object relations in psychoanalytic theory*. Cambridge, MA: Harvard University Press.

Greenson, R. R. 1967. *The technique and practice of psychoanalysis*. New York: International Universities Press.

Gump, J. P. 2000. A white therapist, an African American patient—shame in the therapeutic dyad. *Psychoanalytic Dialogues* 10:619–32.

Howard, G. S. 1991. A narrative approach to thinking, cross-cultural psychology, and psychotherapy. *American Psychologist* 46:187–97.

Jackson, L. C. 2001. The new multiculturalism and psychoanalytic theory: Psychodynamic psychotherapy and African American women. In *Psychotherapy with African American: Innovations in psychodynamic perspectives and practice*, ed. L. C. Jackson and B. G. Greene. New York: Guilford Press.

Jordan, J. V. 1997. A relational perspective for understanding women's development. In *Women's growth in diversity*, ed. J. V. Jordan. New York: Guilford Press.

Kalb, M. B. 2002. Does sex matter? The confluence of gender and transference in analytic space. *Psychoanalytic Psychology* 19:118–43.

Kassam-Adams, N. 1994. *The risks of treating trauma: Stress and secondary trauma in psychotherapists*. Unpublished doctoral dissertation, University of Virginia.

Kazarian, S. S., and D. R. Evans. 1998. *Cultural clinical psychology: Theory, research, and practice*. Oxford: Oxford University Press.

Klein, G. 1976. *Psychoanalytic theory: An exploration of essentials*. New York: International Universities Press.

Kohut, H. 1971. *The analysis of the self*. New York: International Universities Press.

———. 1972. Thoughts on narcissism and narcissistic rage. *The Psychoanalytic Study of the Child* 27:360–400.

———. 1977. *The restoration of the self*. New York: International Universities Press.

Lachmann, F. M., and B. A. Beebe. 1996. Three principles of salience in the organization of the patient-analyst interaction. *Psychoanalytic Psychology* 13:1–22.

———. 1997. Trauma, interpretation, and self-state transformations. *Psychoanalysis and Contemporary Thought* 20:269–91.

Langs, R. J. 1972. The misalliance dimension of the case of the Wolf Man. In *Freud and his patients*, Vol. II, ed. M. Kanzer and J. Glenn, 373–85. New York: Aronson.

Laplanche, J., and J. B. Pontalis. 1973. *The language of psycho-analysis*. New York: W.W. Norton.

Leary, K. 1995. "Interpreting in the dark": Race and ethinicity in psychoanalytic psychotherapy. *Psychoanalytic Psychology* 12:127–40.

———. 1997. Race, self-disclosure, and "forbidden talk": Race and ethnicity in contemporary clinical practice. *Psychoanalytic Quarterly* 66:163–89.

———. 2000. Racial enactments in dynamic treatment. *Psychoanalytic Dialogues* 10:639–53.

———. 2002. Race in psychoanalytic space. In *Gender and analytic space: Between clinic and culture*, ed. M. Dimen and V. Goldner. NewYork: Other Press.

Lichtenberg, J. D., F. M. Lachmann, and J. L. Fosshage. 1992. *Self and motivational systems: Toward a theory of psychoanalytic technique*. Hillsdale, NJ: Analytic Press.

Lipton, S. D. 1977. The advantages of Freud's technique as shown in his analysis of the Rat Man. *International Journal of Psycho-Analysis* 58:255–73.

Loewald, H. W. 1960. On the therapeutic action of psycho-analysis. *International Journal of Psycho-Analysis* 41:16–33.

Lubin, A. J. 1967. The influence of the Russian Orthodox Church on Freud's Wolf Man: An hypothesis. *Psychoanalytic Forum* 2:145–74.

Lyon, E. 1993. Hospital staff reactions to accounts by survivors of childhood abuse. *American Journal of Orthopsychiatry* 63:410–16.

Magid, B. 1993. Self psychology meets the Wolf Man. In *Freud's case studies: Self-psychological perspectives*, ed. B. Magid. Hillsdale, NJ: Analytic Press.

McCann, L., and L. A. Pearlman. 1990. Vicarious traumatization: A framework for understanding the psychological effects of working with victims. *Journal of Traumatic Stress* 3:131–49.

Meissner, W. W. 1977. The Wolf Man and the paranoid process. *The Annual of Psychoanalysis* 5:23–74.

Mio, J. S., and G. Y. Iwamasa. 2003. *Culturally diverse mental health: The challenges of research and resistance*. New York: Brunner-Routledge.

Mishne, J. 2002. *Multiculturalism and the therapeutic process*. New York: Guilford Press.

Mitchell, S. A. 1988. *Relational concepts in psychoanalysis: An integration*. Cambridge, MA: Harvard University Press.

Modell, A. 1984. *Psychoanalysis in a new context*. New York: International Universities Press.

Morrison, A. P. 1989. *Shame: The underside of narcissism*. Hillsdale, NJ: Analytic Press.

———. 1996. *The culture of shame*. New York: Ballantine Books.

Neumann, D. A., and S. J. Gamble. 1995. Issues in the professional development of psychotherapists: Countertransference and vicarious traumatization in the new trauma therapist. *Psychotherapy* 32:341–47.

Obholzer, K. 1982. *The Wolf-Man: Conversations with Freud's controversial patient—Sixty years later*, trans. Michael Shaw. New York: Continuum.

Offenkrantz, W., and A. Tobin. 1973. Problems of the therapeutic alliance: Freud and the Wolf Man. *International Journal of Psycho-Analysis* 54:75–78.

Ogden, T. 1994. *Subjects of analysis*. Northvale, NJ: Jason Aronson.

———. 2001. Re-minding the body. *American Journal of Psychotherapy* 55:92–104.

Orange, D. M. 1995. *Emotional understanding: Studies in psychoanalytic epistemology*. New York: Guilford Press.

———. 2001. From Cartesian minds to experiential worlds in psychoanalysis. *Psychoanalytic Psychology* 18:287–302.

———. 2002. There is no outside: Empathy and authenticity in psychoanalytic process. *Psychoanalytic Psychology* 19:686–700.

———. 2004. The post-Cartesian witness and the psychoanalytic profession. "Workshop Day with Donna M. Orange" for ISIPSe' (Istituto di Specializzazione in Psicologia Psicoanalitica del se' e Psicoanalisi Relazionale), 12–12–98.

Orange, D. M., G. E. Atwood, and R. D. Stolorow. 1997. *Working intersubjectively: Contextualism in psychoanalytic practice*. Hillsdale, NJ: Analytic Press.

Orange, D. M., and R. D. Stolorow. 1998. Self-disclosure from the perspective of intersubjectivity theory. *Psychoanalytic Inquiry* 18:530–37.

Palombo, J. 1985. Depletion states and self object disorders. *Clinical Social Work Journal* 13:32–49.

Pankejeff, S. 1957. Letters pertaining to Freud's "History of an infantile neurosis." *The Psychoanalytic Quarterly* 26:449–60.

———. 1971a. Recollections of my childhood. In *The Wolf-Man by the Wolf-Man*, ed. and trans. M. Gardiner. New York: Basic Books.

———. 1971b. My recollections of Sigmund Freud. In *The Wolf-Man by the Wolf-Man*, ed. and trans. M. Gardiner. New York: Basic Books.

Pearlman L. A., and P. S. MacIan. 1995. Vicarious traumatization: An empirical study of the effects of trauma work on trauma therapists. *Professional Psychology: Research and Practice* 26:558–65.

Pearlman, L. A., and K. W. Saakvitne. 1995. *Trauma and the therapist: Countertransference and vicarious traumatization in psychotherapy with incest survivors*. New York: W.W. Norton.

Perlmutter, L. 1996. Using culture and the intersubjective perspective as a resource: A case study of an African-American couple. *Clinical Social Work Journal* 24:389–401.

Poland, W. S. 2000. Witnessing and otherness. *Journal of the American Psychoanalytic Association* 48:17–34.

Pray, M. 2002. The classical/relational schism and psychic conflict. *Journal of the American Psychoanalytic Association* 50:249–80.

Reckling, A. E., and P. Buirski. 1996. Child abuse, self-development, and affect regulation. *Psychoanalytic Psychology* 13:81–99.

Saakvitne, K. W., L. A. Pearlman, and the Staff of the Traumatic Stress Institute. 1996. *Tranforming the pain: A workbook on vicarious traumatization.* New York: W.W. Norton.

Samuels, A. 1993. *The political psyche.* London: Routledge.

Sandhu, D. S., and C. B. Aspy. 1997. *Counseling for prejudice prevention and reduction.* Alexandria, VA: American Counseling Association.

Schauben, L. J., and P. A. Frazier. 1995. Vicarious trauma: The effects on female counselors of working with sexual violence survivors. *Psychology of Women Quarterly* 19:49–64.

Shane, E. L. 2001. Review of *Making sense together: The intersubjective approach to psychotherapy. Psychologist-Psychoanalyst* 21:52–53.

Shane, M. L., E. Shane, and M. Gales. 1997. *Intimate attachments: Toward a new self psychology.* New York: Guilford Press.

Shapiro, T. 2002. From monologue to dialogue: A transition in psychoanalytic practice. *Journal of the American Psychoanalytic Association* 50:200–19.

Silverman, M. 1987. Clinical material. *Psychoanalytic Inquiry* 7:147–65.

Stern, D. 1985. *The interpersonal world of the infant: A view from psychoanalysis and developmental psychology.* New York: Basic Books.

Stern, D., L. Sander, J. Nahum, A. Harrison, N. Bruschweiler-Stern, and E. Tronick. 1998. Non-interpretive mechanisms in psychoanalytic therapy. *International Journal of Psycho-Analysis* 79:903–21.

Stolorow, R. D. 1978. The concept of psychic structure: Its metapsychological and clinical psychoanalytic meanings. *International Review of Psycho-Analysis* 5:313–20.

———. 1994. The nature and therapeutic action of psychoanalytic interpretation. In *The intersubjective perspective*, ed. R. D. Stolorow, G. E. Atwood, and B. Brandchaft. Northvale, NJ: Jason Aronson.

———. 1997. Dynamic, dyadic, intersubjective systems: An evolving paradigm for psychoanalysis. *Psychoanalytic Psychology* 14:337–46.

Stolorow, R. D., and G. E. Atwood. 1992. *Contexts of being: The intersubjective foundations of psychological life.* Hillsdale, NJ: Analytic Press.

Stolorow, R. D., G. E. Atwood, and D. M. Orange. 2002. *Worlds of experience: interweaving philosophical and clinical dimensions in psychoanalysis.* New York: Basic Books.

Stolorow, R. D., G. E. Atwood, and J. L. Trop. 1992. Varieties of therapeutic impasse. In *Contexts of being: The intersubjective foundations of psychological life*, ed. R. D. Stolorow and G. E. Atwood, 104–22. Hillsdale, NJ: Analytic Press.

Stolorow, R. D., B. Brandchaft, and G. E. Atwood. 1987. *Psychoanalytic treatment: An intersubjective approach.* Hillsdale, NJ: Analytic Press.

Stolorow, R. D., and F. M. Lachmann. 1984/1985. Transference: The future of an illusion. *The Annual of Psychoanalysis* 12/13:19–37. Madison, CT: International Universities Press.

Stolorow, R. D., D. M. Orange, and G. E. Atwood. 2001. Cartesian and post-Cartesian trends in relational psychoanalysis. *Psychoanalytic Psychology* 18:468–84.

Stuart, R. B. 2004. Twelve practical suggestions for achieving multicultural competence. *Professional Psychology: Research and Practice* 35:3–8.

Sue, D. W., and D. Sue. 1999. *Counseling the culturally different: Theory and practice.* 3rd ed. New York: Wiley.

Szajnberg, N. M. 1994. Bruno Bettelheim: Culture in man, man in culture, and a language for both. *Psychoanalytic Review* 81:491–507.

Teicholz, J. G. 1999. *Kohut, Loewald, and the postmoderns: A comparative study of self and relationship.* Hillsdale, NJ: Analytic Press.

———. 2001. The many meanings of intersubjectivity and their implications for analyst self-expression and self-disclosure. In *The narcissistic patient revisited: Progress in self psychology,* Vol. 7, ed. A. Golberg, 9–42. Hillsdale, NJ: Analytic Press.

Thelen, E., and L. Smith. 1994. *A dynamic systems approach to the development of cognition and action.* Cambridge, MA: MIT Press.

Thomas, K. R. 1992. The Wolf-Man case: Classical and self-psychological perspectives. *The American Journal of Psychoanalysis* 52:213–25.

Tosone, C., L. Bialkin, M. Campbell, M. Charters, K. Gieri, S. Gross, C. Grounds, K. Johnson, D. Kitson, S. Lanzo, M. Lee, M. Martinez, M. M. Martinez, J. Millich, A. Riofrio, L. Rosenblatt, J. Sandler, M. Scali, M. Spiro, and A. Stefan. 2003. Shared trauma: Group reflections on the September 11th disaster. *Psychoanalytic Social Work* 10:57–77.

Toukmanian, S. G., and M. C. Brouwers. 1998. Cultural aspects of self-disclosure and psychotherapy. In *Culturally diverse mental health: The challenges of research and resistance,* ed. J. S. Mio and G. Y. Iwamasa. New York: Brunner-Routledge.

van der Kolk, B. 2000. Trauma, neuroscience and the etiology of hysteria: An exploration of the relevance of Breuer and Freud's 1893 article in light of modern science. *Journal of the American Academy of Psychoanalysis* 28:237–62.

Wasserman, M. D. 1999. The impact of psychoanalytic theory and a two-person psychology on the empathizing analyst. *International Journal of Psychoanalysis* 80:464–99.

White, K. 2002. Surviving hating and being hated: Some personal thoughts about racism from a psychoanalytic perspective. *Contemporary Psychoanalysis* 38:401–22.

Winnicott, D. W. 1965. *The maturational process and the facilitating environment.* New York: International Universities Press.

Wolf, E. 1988. *Treating the self.* New York: Guilford Press.

Wortis, J. 1954. *Fragments of an analysis with Freud.* New York: Simon & Schuster.

Yi, K. Y. 1998. Transference and race: An intersubjective conceptualization. *Psychoanalytic Psychology* 15:245–61.

Young-Bruehl, E. 1996. *The anatomy of prejudices.* Cambridge, MA: Harvard University Press.

Zeddies, T. J. 2000. Within, outside, and in between: The relational unconscious. *Psychoanalytic Psychology* 17:467–87.

Zetzel, E. R. 1956. Current concepts of transference. *International Journal of Psychoanalysis* 37:369–76.

Index

About the Author and Coauthors

Peter Buirski, PhD, is dean of the Graduate School of Professional Psychology at the University of Denver and clinical professor of psychiatry at the University of Colorado Health Sciences Center. He holds the Diplomate in Clinical Psychology and in Psychoanalysis from the American Board of Professional Psychology, and maintains a private practice in Denver. He is the coauthor of the book, *Making Sense Together: The Intersubjective Approach to Psychotherapy* and has written on the psychotherapy process as well as on primate personality.

Michelle Doft, PsyD, works in a group practice in Denver, Colorado, conducting both individual and group therapy.

Pamela Haglund, PsyD, is a candidate at the Denver Institute for Psychoanalysis. She is the coauthor of *Making Sense Together: The Intersubjective Approach to Psychotherapy* and is in private practice.

Martha Kendall Ryan, PsyD, is in private practice in Denver, Colorado, specializing in psychotherapy with individuals and couples.

Erin Shrago, PsyD, is in private practice in Denver, Colorado, where she sees adults and adolescents. Additionally, she performs psychological testing as well as learning evaluations for all age groups.